There Really is a

Santa Claus

The History of Saint Nicholas & Christmas Holiday Traditions

William J. Federer

ISBN 0-9653557-4-8   Library of Congress HISTORY/EDUCATION

Picture Credits:
The Menil Collection, USA Today, December 23, 1997, 1A-2A
Netherlands Information Service, Particam, Amsterdam
Thomas Nast, Illustrator, Harper's Weekly Magazine
Haddon Sundblom, Illustrator, Coca-Cola Bottling Company
Norman Rockwell, Illustrator, Saturday Evening Post
Benjamin R. Hanby, Illustrator
http://www.provenceguide.com/Agenda/Noel/creche.jpg
http://www2.egenet.com.tr/mastersj/ottoman-henry-viii-wives.jpg
http://www.bantams.demon.co.uk/Martin%20Luther.jpg
http://home.attbi.com/~histotech2/stnicholas.jpg
http://users.newburyweb.net/n1012925/virtual_tour/images/
Window%2005.jpg
H. Armstrong Roberts, Inc.
Hallmark Cards
The Bettmann Archive
New York Public Library Picture Collection

Special thanks to Dr. Jerry Newcombe and Dr. Jack Kinneer
for Biblical and historical research as to the date of the Nativity.

FREE EBOOK
As owner of this book, you can receive as a
limited-time offer a free ebook of this title.
Email: **wjfederer@gmail.com** with subject line SANTA 2011
and the ebook (pdf file) will be attached to a reply email.

Amerisearch, Inc., P.O. Box 20163, St. Louis, MO 63123
1-888-USA-WORD, 314-487-4395 voice/fax
www.amerisearch.net, wjfederer@gmail.com

Dedicated to Melody Federer
"Our Christmas Baby"

- Charles Dickens
A Christmas Carol, 1843

"...and it was always said of him,
that he knew how to keep Christmas well,
if any man alive possessed the knowledge.
May that be truly said of us, and all of us!
And so, as Tiny Tim observed,
'God bless Us, Every One!'"

Contents

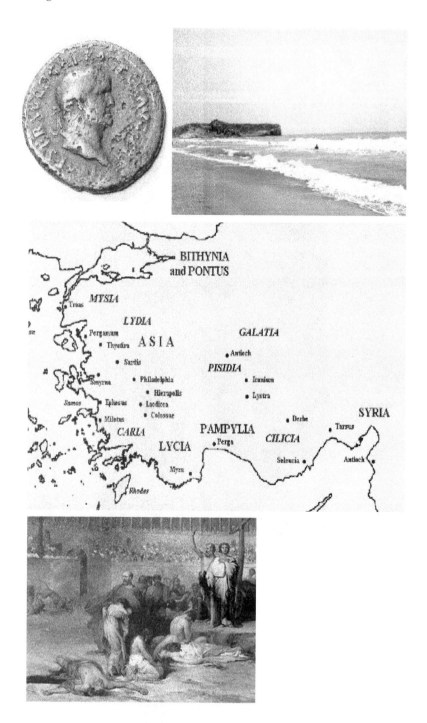

ORIGINS

𝕿he year was 280 AD.

This was twenty-one years prior to Armenia's King, Tiridates the Great, rejecting Persian Zoroastrianism and local polytheist pagan religions, and declaring Christianity as his country's official state religion, the first nation ever to do so.

It was twenty-two years prior to the violent persecution of Christians by Roman Emperor Diocletian, which was the worst of the ten major persecutions during Christianity's first 300 years.

It was also thirty-three years prior to Roman Emperor Constantine's grant of official toleration to the Christian religion in 313 AD.

This same year, 280 AD, in the town of Patara, located in the region of Lycia, Asia Minor, (present-day Turkey) a child was born to a wealthy, elderly couple who had been unable to have children. The child was named Nicholas.

All legend is based in some fact, and the facts which history records is that in the 3rd-4th Century, there lived a person of reputation named Nicholas on the northeast coast of the Mediterranean Sea in an area known as Asia Minor; that he was significant enough to be made a Bishop and spiritual enough to be called by the title Saint.

In researching the background of Saint Nicholas, many sources had bits and pieces of the stories of his life, but the record passed down by the Greek Orthodox Church appears to elaborate the most on the details of his career. This would appear appropriate, as Nicholas lived in that area

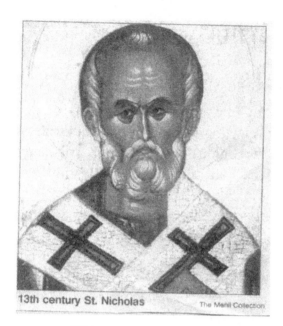

13th century St. Nicholas   The Menil Collection

There Really is a Santa Claus

of the world. Some would contend that this history is mixed with legend, but being unqualified to distinguish between the two, this author has decided to relate the essence of the story as received.

THE STORY

𝔄ccordingly to the Greek Orthodox history, Nicholas' parents, Theophanes and Nonna, received him as their son after many years of prayer, similar to Abraham and Sarah of the Bible. They considered this child a direct gift from God with a special calling to help people. They therefore named him "Nicholas," which meant in Greek "victor or hero of the people."

Even as an infant, Nicholas displayed remarkable instances of a special call on his life. As he grew, he was known for his virtue, especially in the study of scripture, abstinence and temperance. He began fasting every Wednesday and Friday, a habit which he continued throughout his life. He was chaste and pure in his thoughts, sometimes spending entire days and nights in church praying and reading divine books.

The bishop of the town of Patara was Nicholas' uncle, whom Nicholas was named after. He noticed how Nicholas avoided worldly pursuits and therefore advised his parents that their son may be called to the service of God. Nicholas then entered the nearby monastery of Sion and trained for the ministry under his uncle. When Nicholas was ordained, his uncle pronounced a prophecy:

I see, brethren, a new sun rising above
the earth and manifesting in himself a gracious

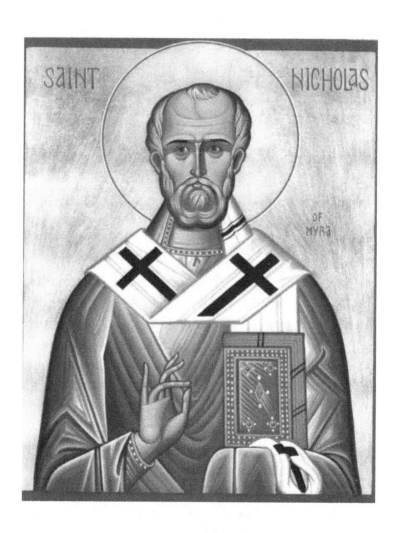

consolation for the afflicted. Blessed is the flock that will be worthy to have him as its pastor, because this one will shepherd well the souls of those who have gone astray, will nourish them on the pasturage of piety, and will be a merciful helper in misfortune and tribulation.

As time went on his uncle, the Bishop, desired to go on pilgrimage to the Holy Land. He handed oversight of the church to his nephew Nicholas. Nicholas was known for keeping all night vigils, remaining unceasing in prayer and fasting. He took the responsibility of the church seriously and cared for the congregation the same way the Bishop had.

It was at this time that Nicholas' parents died during a plague, leaving him a substantial inheritance. He was very generous in distributing it to the poor and needy, feeding the hungry, clothing the naked and ransoming those taken captive by debt to moneylenders.

SECRET GIFT-GIVING OF ST. NICHOLAS

ℛicholas is most notably remembered for helping the family of a nobleman of Patara who had gone bankrupt. Ruthless creditors not only took the nobleman's property, but threatened to take his three beautiful daughters as well. The father's only hope was to marry off his daughters quickly before the creditors could take them, thereby saving them from a life of white slavery and prostitution. Unfortunately, he did not have money for the girls' dowries, which were necessary for them to marry.

Nicholas heard of this dilemma and late one night threw a bag of gold in the family's window to save the eldest daughter from the fate of an outcast. The news spread across town and she was soon lawfully married. Shortly thereafter, Nicholas did the same, rescuing the second daughter. The father is said to have exclaimed:

O merciful God, Author of our salvation, Who hast redeemed me by Thine Own Blood and now redeemest by gold my home and my daughters from the nets of the enemy, do Thou Thyself show me the minister of Thy mercy and Thy philanthropic goodness.

Show me this earthly angel who preserves us from sinful perdition, so that I might know who hath snatched us from poverty which oppresses us and delivers us from evil thoughts and intentions.

O Lord, by Thy mercy secretly done for me by the generous hand of Thy servant unknown to me, I can give my second daughter lawfully in marriage and with this escape the snares of the devil, who desired by a tainted gain, or even without it, to increase my great ruin.

Finally, when Nicholas threw the bag of gold in to save the third daughter, which supposedly landed in one of her stockings set out by the fireplace to dry, the father ran outside and caught him, saying:

If the Lord great in mercy had not raised me up through thy generosity, then I,

an unfortunate father, already long ago would he lost together with my daughters in the fire of Sodom. Now we are saved through thee and delivered from a horrible fall into sin.

Nicholas, who wanted the glory to go to God alone, made the father swear with an oath not to reveal where the gifts came from while Nicholas was living.

This was the basis for the later tradition of secret gift-giving on the anniversary of Nicholas' death.

PATRON SAINT OF PAWNBROKERS

The story of his coming to the rescue of a family in financial need led to Saint Nicholas being considered the "Patron Saint of Pawn Brokers," as they lend to families in times of financial need.

The three bags of gold that Saint Nicholas threw in the window led bankers, moneylenders and pawnbrokers to adopt "three gold balls" as their symbol.

TRIP TO THE HOLY LAND

After several years, Nicholas desired to go to the Holy Land to see the places where Jesus walked. He boarded a ship which sailed first across the Mediterranean to North Africa and then set course for Palestine. As the ship was passing Egypt, Nicholas perceived that a storm would soon arise and warned his fellow travelers, telling them that it was as if he saw the devil himself enter the ship with the

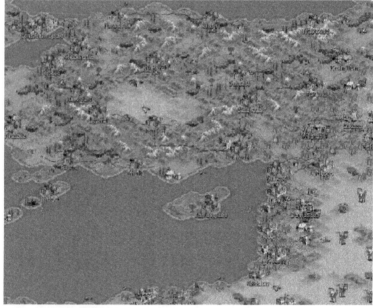

intent to drown them in the depths the hour, the heavens grew black with clouds and the sea raged in a terrible storm. The travelers, certain of death, called out to Nicholas:

> If thou, O servant of God, do not help us by thy prayers to the Lord, then we shall immediately perish.

Nicholas commanded them to have courage and trust God for a speedy deliverance. As Nicholas prayed fervently, the sea quickly became peaceful. A sailor, though, slipped and fell from the top of the mast and lay dead on the deck. Nicholas immediately prayed for him and the sailor arose as if awakening from sleep.

Their ship arrived at Alexandria, North Africa, where Nicholas consoled the afflicted and prayed for many ill and possessed people who were subsequently healed. Finally Nicholas resumed his journey to the Holy Land.

Arriving at Jerusalem, Nicholas visited Golgotha, where Christ was crucified, and the other holy places. The Greek Orthodox history states:

> And when at night he wanted to enter a holy church for prayer, the closed doors of the church swung open by themselves, disclosing an unhindered entry to him for whom were opened also the heavenly gates.

LEAVING JERUSALEM

After spending long enough in Jerusalem, Nicholas intended to journey into the desert and there dedicate himself

to a life of solitude and prayer, but "a Divine voice from on high" instructed him to return to his homeland and not hide his light under a bushel.

Nicholas boarded a ship to return to his homeland of Lycia, but after they departed, the crew set course in a different direction. Nicholas fell at their feet and beseeched them to change their direction, but they refused. Suddenly a storm arose and threatened the ship with destruction, and in the course blew the ship around toward Lycia.

MONASTERY OF SION

Once again in the region of Lycia, Nicholas came to the Monastery of Holy Sion, which had been founded by his uncle the Bishop. A welcome guest to the brotherhood, they received him as an angel and were encouraged by his divinely inspired speeches. Nicholas seriously considered consecrating himself to the peaceful contemplative life of the monastery, but was admonished not to bury his treasure by a voice heard while standing at prayer:

> Nicholas, if you desire to be vouchsafed a crown from me, go and struggle for the good of the world.

As Nicholas pondered this, he heard again:

> Nicholas, here is not the field on which you must bring forth the fruit I expect, but turn back and go into the world and let My name be glorified in you.

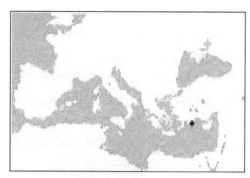

There Really is a Santa Claus

Nicholas decided to leave the monastery. Instead of returning to the Patara, the city of his birth, he chose to go where he was unknown, to the large coastal metropolis of Myra.

BECOMING A BISHOP

𝔄rriving there, Nicholas lived as a pauper, having nowhere to lay his head. His only refuge was the house of the Lord. As providence would have it, John, the archbishop of the entire land of Lycia, had died.

Bishops from the entire region gathered in Myra to choose a replacement. There was great discord, as no agreement could be made. One of their number stood up and proclaimed:

> The election of a bishop to this throne
> is not up to the decision of people, but is a
> matter of God's direction. It is proper for us
> to say prayers so that the Lord Himself will
> disclose who is worthy to receive such rank
> and be the shepherd of the whole land of
> Lycia.

The council responded by devoting themselves to prayer and fasting. After a few days, the eldest bishop saw a vision while standing at prayer.

Before him appeared a man in an image of light and commanded him to go to the doors of the church during the night and observe who would enter before everyone else.

"This" said He, "is my choice; receive him with honor and install him as archbishop; the name of this man is Nicholas."

The bishop informed the entire council, who increased their prayers. The eldest bishop stationed himself all night by the church doors in anticipation. When time came for the morning service, Nicholas, who had been accustomed to rise at midnight for prayer, arrived at church before all others.

As soon as Nicholas entered the church, the elderly bishop stopped him and asked his name. Nicholas remained silent. The bishop asked again, and Nicholas meekly and softly answered him:

> My name is Nicholas, I am the servant
> of thy holiness, Master.

The bishop, hearing the name "Nicholas" and beholding his humble and meek manner, rejoiced and took Nicholas by the hand saying: "Follow me, child."

The other bishops were immediately delighted and relieved that the vacant archbishop position was to be filled. Word of this instantly spread everywhere and multitudes of people began flocking to the church. The elderly bishop addressed the crowd:

> Brethren, receive your shepherd
> whom the Holy Spirit Himself anointed and
> to whom He entrusted the care of your souls.
> He was not appointed by an assembly of men,
> but by God Himself.
> Now we have the one that we desired,
> and have found and accepted the one we

sought. Under his rule and instruction we will not lack the hope that we will stand before God in the day of His appearing and revelation.

For a quite a while Nicholas refused the office, being unable to endure the praise of men, but after ardent requests from the council of bishops, he remembered a vision he had prior to the death of archbishop John, and yielded to ascend the episcopal throne against his will.

Nicholas strove to be an example to the believers, in word, in conversation, in love, in spirit, in faith, and in purity. He was humble of spirit and forgiving, shunning all vainglory. He wore simple clothing and ate only once a day - in the evening.

All the day long he spent in labor proper to his office, listening to the requests and needs of those who came to him. The doors of his house were open to all. He was kind and affable to all, to orphans he was a father, to the poor a merciful giver, to the weeping a comforter, to the wronged a helper, and to all a great benefactor.

NICHOLAS PERSECUTED

There were 11 major persecutions of Christians by Roman Emperors in the first 400 years:

64-68 AD	Nero
89-96 AD	Domitian
109-117 AD	Trajan
161-180 AD	Marcus Aurelius
193-211 AD	Septimius Severus

235-238 AD	Maximinus the Thracian
249-251 AD	Decius
253-260 AD	Valerian
285-305 AD	Diocletian
305-313 AD	Galerius
361-363 AD	Julian the Apostate

During the life of Nicholas, persecution arose against the Church from Emperor Diocletian and his co-regent Maximian. These two rulers of the East held a council at Nicomedia in 302 AD and resolved to suppress Christianity throughout the empire.

On February 24, 303 AD, they demolished the cathedral of Nicomedia.

An edict was issued "to tear down the churches to the foundations and to destroy the Sacred Scriptures by fire; and commanding also that those who were in honourable stations should be degraded if they persevered in their adherence to Christianity" (Eusebius, op. cit., VIII, ii).

Three further edicts, between 303-304 AD, marked successive stages in the severity of the persecution: the first ordering that the bishops, presbyters, and deacons should be imprisoned; the second that they should be tortured and compelled by every means to sacrifice; the third including the laity as well as the clergy.

The atrocious cruelty with which these edicts were enforced, and the vast numbers of those who suffered for the Faith are attested by the historian Eusebius and in the Acts of the Martyrs. An order was sent throughout the Roman Empire that Christians must renounce Christ and worship idols. Those who did not submit to this order were compelled to it by confinement in prison and severe torture and, finally, given over to execution. In some cases, whole

populations of towns were massacred because they declared themselves Christians (Eusebius, loc. cit., xi, xii; Lactant., "Div. Instit.", V, xi).

On May 1, 305 AD, Emperor Diocletian abdicated his throne, in part because of a painful intestinal illness. This was unprecedented for a Roman Emperor to resign and soon there was partial relief from the persecution. In the Eastern part of the Empire, however, where Galerius and Maximian held sway, the persecution continued to rage. Therefore the so-called Diocletian persecution should be attributed to the influence of Galerius, who continued it for seven years after Diocletian's abdication.

This storm of persecution had quickly reached Myra.

Bishop Nicholas, who was the leader of all Christians in the city, continued freely and boldly to preach the piety of Christ, despite threats of suffering. He was soon seized by torturers and confined in prison with many other Christians. He remained there for several years, bearing severe suffering, and enduring hunger and thirst in the overcrowded dungeon. He ministered to his fellow prisoners and encouraged them to stand strong in their faith in Christ.

When Galerius died, the leadership of Rome fell into dispute. After several battles, it came down to Constantine and Maxentius fighting for control of the entire Empire.

"X" – MAS

𝕵ust prior to the fateful contest, Constantine saw a sign of Christ in the sky. It reportedly was the first two letters of the Greek name for Christ. The first letter, written "X" is called "Chi" and the second letter "P" is called "Rho." Constantine saw with the "Chi-Rho" the words "In Hoc Signa

There Really is a Santa Claus

Vinces," which interpreted means, "In This Sign You Will Be Victorious."

Constantine had his soldiers put this Christian sign on all his flags and standards. When he won the Battle of the Milvian Bridge, he ordered all persecution of Christians to cease.

The "Chi-Rho" - XP was shortened to simply "Chi." In 1390, the mark + or X written before the alphabet was called the Cros-Kryst, meaning the Cross of Christ.

In 1475 this evolved into the Middle English pronunciation of "Christ's-Cross" or "Criss-Cross."

Learning the "Criss-Cross Row," was the expression used for learning the alphabet. The mark "X" stood for the phrase Christ-cross me speed ("May Christ's Cross give me success"), an invocation said before reciting the alphabet.

The Criss-Cross or Christ's-Cross "X" was also a form of written oath before God used when signing one's name on a document, similar to swearing upon a Bible and saying "so help me God."

In the event a person could not write, signing the "Christ's-Cross" was used in place of their signature and often accompanied with a kiss to show sincerity.

This is the origin of putting X's and O's on the bottom of St. Valentine's Day Cards to express a pledge before God sealed with a kiss. It was also the origin of Medieval practice of "crossing one's heart."

EDICT OF TOLERATION & ST. NICHOLAS FREED

"St. Paul at Ephesus" by Gustave Doré

Shortly thereafter, in 313 AD, the new Emperor Constantine issued the Edict of Toleration.

This officially gave Christianity tolerance throughout the Roman Empire. Constantine ordered the release of those imprisoned for Christ. He honored them with great praises and allowed them to return to their homelands. At this time Bishop Nicholas was allowed to return to the city of Myra and was joyously received back as its beloved shepherd.

CONFRONTING PAGANISM

At that time there still remained many Hellenic temples, to which numerous inhabitants in the area around Myra were attracted for their lustful and immoral ceremonies with temple prostitutes, animal divination, infant exposure and human sacrifice.

Bishop Nicholas preached against these idol temples, resulting in the people tearing down the local temple of Diana. His preaching, along with John Chrysostom, resulted in the people tearing down the main Temple of Diana at Ephesus, which the Apostle Paul had also preached against as recorded in the Book of Acts, chapter 19. It had been one of the seven wonders of the ancient world with 127 huge pillars, and served as the center of a kind of Las Vegas style immorality cult for the Mediterranean.

COUNCIL OF NICEA

Emperor Constantine embraced Christianity and desired to end the Arian heresy which was splitting the church. He commanded, in the year 325 AD, that an

ecumenical council be convened in Nicea, a city just 300 miles from Myra. There were 318 church leaders attending from the all over the Roman world, and among them was Bishop Nicholas.

The council ended the Arian heresy, which demoted Jesus to "less than" God, and in its place affirmed the divinity of Christ, the three persons of the Trinity, and that the Son of God was of equal honor, essence, and co-everlasting with the Father. The council produced the Nicene Creed, a popular profession of faith which is used in churches throughout the world. At a critical moment during the council, Nicholas boldly stood up to Arius.

A monk, John, of the Studite Monastery, related that Nicholas, "animated like the prophet Elias with zeal for God, put the heretic Arius to shame at the council not only by word but also by deed, smiting him on the cheek."

The fathers of the council, indignant at Nicholas for his daring action, decided to deprive him of his episcopal rank. But before the council ended, some of the holy fathers of the council had a vision similar to the one Nicholas himself had before he was ordained back in Myra. They ceased to reprove him and returned to him the emblems of his rank.

Returning from the council to his flock, Nicholas strove to care for the needs of his people and endeavored to diligently teach the truth of scripture.

STORIES OF SAINT NICHOLAS

Once he was reported to have prayed for a baby, preventing it from being burnt after scalding water had been accidentally spilt on it. Another time he made the sign of

the cross over an insane, uncontrollable boy and the boy became sound of mind.

Once there was a famine in the land of Lycia so severe that people were starving. Bishop Nicholas responded to the situation by going down to the docks and asking some ships from Alexandria, North Africa, which were bound for Rome, to unload some of their grain to help his people. He promised the sailors that whatever they gave, God would restore it to them before they reached their destination. On their return trip, the sailors reported that the Bishop's word had been fulfilled!

During another famine the city of Myra had an extreme food shortage. Bishop Nicholas set himself to prayer. It then happened that one night a certain merchant far away in Italy with a ship loaded with grain for another land, had a dream. He dreamt of Bishop Nicholas commanding him to sail to Myra and giving him three gold coins as a pledge. When he awoke, he was frightened to find three gold coins in his hand. The merchant dared not disobey the dream and sailed for the city of Myra, where he sold his grain to its inhabitants, relieving their hunger and captivating them with his tale.

PATRON SAINT OF SAILORS

𝔑umerous times, storms arose in the port city of Myra that were so violent that ships were unable to return to shore. The inhabitants would get Bishop Nicholas to come down to the docks and pray for the seas to become calm. His prayers were answered and the boats could return to shore safely. This resulted in St. Nicholas later being considered the "Patron Saint of Sailors."

There was another story somewhat to the effect that Bishop Nicholas miraculously rescued three youths who were about to be murdered and put into a large vat of brine.

RESCUING THE INNOCENT

𝔄t that time in the region of Phrygia there arose a revolt. Having learned of it, Emperor Constantine sent three commanders with their soldiers to pacify the rebellion. The commanders: Nepotian, Ursus, and Herpylion, set sail in haste from Constantinople. Rough seas forced them to find shelter along the Adriatic shore at a port in Lycia.

As they remained there waiting for the season of bad weather to pass, certain soldiers went ashore to purchase necessities and ended up taking a great deal by force. Evidently, this happened frequently to port cities and the embittered inhabitants gathered at a place called Plakomata to confront the soldiers.

Hearing of this impending riot in an area under his oversight, Bishop Nicholas traveled the distance there to quell the strife. Upon his arrival, the citizens, together with the soldiers, went out to meet him and bowed down. Nicholas asked the commanders whence and whither they guarded the way. They told him that they were sent by the emperor to Phrygia to put down the revolt which had arisen there.

Nicholas admonished them to hold their soldiers in submission and not to allow them to oppress the people. After this he invited the commanders into the city and cordially entertained them. The commanders, having disciplined the offending soldiers, stilled the revolt, and were honored with a blessing from Nicholas.

As this was incident was concluding, there arrived from Myra several citizens lamenting and weeping. They fell at Nicholas' feet and begged him to return at once to defend three innocent men who were condemned to die by the bribed ruler Eustathius:

> Our whole town laments and weeps,
> and awaits your return, Master. For if you had
> been with us, then the ruler would not have
> dared to make such an unjust judgment.

Hearing this, Nicholas grieved in his soul and from the company of the commanders he immediately set out. Upon reaching a place, called "Leo," they met certain travelers and asked whether they knew of those men condemned to death. They answered:

> We fell them on the field of Castor
> and Pollux, being dragged away to execution
> pressed on faster, rushing to prevent the death
> of the innocent men.

Having reached the place of execution, he saw a multitude gathered there with the condemned men bound crosswise. They were kneeling on the ground with their bare necks stretched out, waiting the blow of the executioner's sword, which had already been drawn.

Into the midst of this spectacle of horror and distress, Nicholas went. Combining anger with meekness, he freely passed among the crowd and without fear approached executioner and snatched the sword from his hands and threw it upon the ground. He then set the condemned men free of their bonds.

The men, seeing themselves unexpectedly restored from near death to life, shed warm tears and uttered joyful cries, and the all the people assembled there gave thanks to their bishop. When ruler Eustathius arrived and wanted to approach the bishop, Nicholas turned away from him with disdain.

The ruler fell toward him, but Nicholas thrust him aside, calling down the wrath of God upon him for his unjust rule and promised to tell the emperor of his deeds. Being denounced by his own conscience and frightened by the threats of the bishop, the ruler with tears begged for mercy. Repenting of his injustice and desiring reconciliation with the great Father Nicholas, he laid his guilt before the elders of the city, Simonides and Eudocius.

But the lie could not be hid, because Nicholas knew well that the ruler, being bribed with gold, condemned the innocent to death. For a long time the ruler begged Nicholas to forgive him, and only then, when, with great humility and tears he acknowledged his sin, did Nicholas grant him forgiveness.

Returning to the story of the three commanders whom Nicholas met with in Lycia, they set out for Phrygia and quickly suppressed the revolt. Having fulfilled their royal commission, they returned with joy to Byzantium.

The emperors and all the grandees gave them great praise and honor, and they were deemed worthy to take part in the royal council. But evil people envying such fame of the commanders, conceived enmity against them. They came to Eulavius, the ruler of the city, and slandered those men, saying:

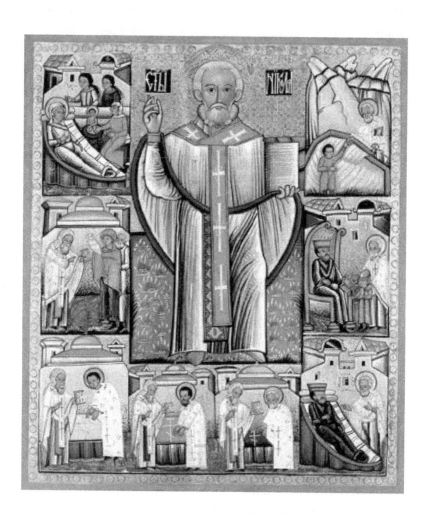

The commanders counsel ill, because,
as we have heard, they introduce innovations
and mediate evil against the emperor.

In order to win over the ruler to their side, they gave
him much gold. The ruler informed the emperor. Having heard
about this, the emperor, without any investigation, ordered
those commanders to be confined in prison, learning that
they might run away secretly and fulfill their evil design.

Languishing in jail, and conscious of their innocence,
the commanders were perplexed as to why they were
imprisoned.

After a short time, the slanderers began to fear that
their evil would come to light and they themselves might
suffer. They came to the ruler and fervently begged him not
to allow those men to live long and to quickly condemn them
to death. Ensnared in the nets of avarice, the ruler was
obliged to carry out what was promised to the end.

He immediately departed to the emperor and, like a
messenger of evil, appeared before him with a sad face and
a sorrowful look. Along with this, he wished to show that he
was very much concerned about the life of the emperor and
truly devoted to him. Striving to incite the emperor's anger
against the innocent, he began to hold forth with lying and
cunning speech, saving:

O Emperor, not one of those shut in
prison wishes to repent. All of them persist
in their evil design, not ceasing to plot
intrigues against you. Therefore, command
without delay to hand them over to torture,
so that they may not anticipate us and

"St. Nicholas with Saints" 18th C. Rus. - The Elsner Collection

accomplish their evil deed, which they planned against the military commanders and you.

Alarmed by these words the emperor immediately condemned the commanders to death. But because it was evening, their punishment was delayed until morning. The prison guard learned of this. Having privately shed many tears over such a disaster threatening the innocent, he went to the commanders and said to them:

> For me it would have been better if I had not known you and had not enjoyed pleasant conversation and repast with you. Then I would easily bear separation from you and would not lament in soul over the disaster coming upon you.
>
> Morning will come, and the final and horrible separation will overtake us. I already do not see your faces dear to me, and do not hear your voice, because the emperor ordered to execute you. Instruct me how to deal with your possessions while there is yet time, and death has not yet prevented you from expressing your will.

He interrupted his speech with sobs. When the generals learned of their horrible sentence, they rent their clothing and tore their hair, saying:

> What enemy has begrudged us our lives? For the sake of what are we, like malefactors, condemned to execution? What

have we done, for what is it necessary to hand
us over to death?

And they called upon their relatives and friends by
name, setting God Himself as their witness, that they had
done no evil, and wept bitterly. One of them by the name of
Nepotian recalled how they were rescued.

The commanders began to pray:

O God of Nicholas, having delivered
the three men from an unjust death, look now
also upon us, for there can be no help from
men. There hath come upon us a great disaster,
and there is none who might deliver us from
disaster.

Our voice is cut off before the
departure of our soul from the body, and our
tongue is parched, burnt up by the fire of our
heartfelt distress, so that we are not able to
offer prayer unto Thee. Let Thy compassions
quickly go before us, O Lord. Rescue us out
the hand of them that seek after our souls.

Tomorrow they wish to kill us, but do
Thou hasten to our aid and deliver us innocent
ones from death.

Later that night, as the Emperor slept, he had a dream
in which he saw Nicholas telling him:

Arise quickly and release those
commanders languishing in prison. They were
slandered to you and they suffer guiltlessly.

In the dream, Nicholas explained the plot and added:

> If you do not obey me and do not let
> them go, then I will raise a revolt against you
> similar to the one that occurred in Phrygia
> and you will perish by an evil death.

Astounded at such boldness, the emperor, in the dream, began to wonder how this man dared to enter into his inner chamber at night, and said to him:

> Who are you that you dare to threaten
> us and our power?

He replied:

> My name is Nicholas, I am the bishop
> of the metropolis of Myra.

The emperor became confused and, arising, began to ponder upon what this dream meant. Meanwhile, on that same night, the ruler Eulavius awoke from having the exact same dream. As he was pondering it, there came a messenger from the emperor and telling him of the emperor's dream.

Hastening to the emperor, the ruler disclosed what he saw in his dream and both of them were amazed that they had seen one and the same thing. At once the emperor ordered the commanders brought to him from prison, and said to them:

> By what sorcery did you bring these
> dreams upon us? A very angry man appeared

to us and threatened us, boasting to soon bring
war upon us.

The commanders turned one to another in perplexity
and, knowing nothing, looked at one another with distressed
glances. Noticing this, the emperor was mollified and said:
"Fear no evil, tell the truth."

With tears and sobs they replied:

Emperor, we know nothing of sorcery
and have designed no evil against your power,
may the All-seeing Lord be a witness in this.
If we are deceiving you, and you learn anything
ill of us, then allow no favor or clemency
either to us or to our relatives. From our
fathers we learned to honor the emperor and
be faithful to him before all things.

Thus also now we faithfully defend
your life and, as is proper to our rank,
unswervingly fulfill your commands to us.
Serving you with zeal, we subdued the revolt
in Phrygia, stopped the civil strife, and
demonstrated our courage sufficiently by this
deed itself, as those witness to whom this is
well-known.

Your power heaped honors upon us
before, and now you with anger set yourself
against us and pitilessly condemned us to an
agonizing death.

And so, O Emperor, we think that we
suffer only for our zeal toward you alone, for
which we have been condemned and, instead

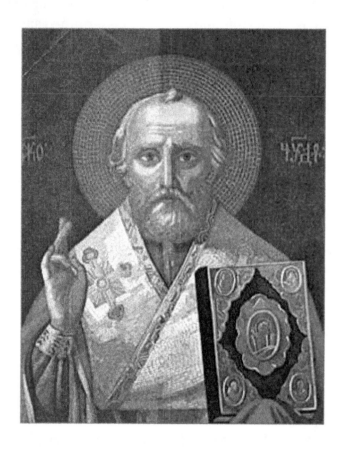

of glory and honors which we had hoped to receive, the fear of death has overtaken us.

At this address the emperor became compassionate and repented of his rash behavior. For he began to tremble before the judgment of God and felt embarrassment for his royal purple, seeing that he, being a lawgiver for others, was ready to make a lawless judgment. He looked compassionately upon the condemned men and conversed with them briefly, asking them:

> Who is this Nicholas, and which men did he save? Tell me about it.

Nepotian related to him everything in the order of its occurrence. Then the emperor, learning that Nicholas was a great man of God, marveled at his boldness and his great zeal in defense of the wronged, freed those commanders and said to them:

> It is not I that grants you life, but the great servant of the Lord, Nicholas, whom you called upon for help. Go to him and offer him thanksgiving. Say to him also from me that "I fulfilled your command that the servant of Christ be not angry with me."

With these words he handed them a golden Gospel, a golden censer ornamented with stones and two lamps, and ordered all this to be given to the church of Myra. Having received a miraculous escape, the commanders set out on their way at once. Arriving in Myra, they rejoiced and were

glad that they were vouchsafed to see Nicholas again. They expressed great gratitude in prayer, saying:

> Lord, O Lord, who is like unto Thee?
> Delivering the beggar from the hand of them
> that are stronger than he.

They gave generous alms to the needy and paupers, and returned home safely. Such are the stories from which the fame of Nicholas spread everywhere, even across the sea, so that there was no place where people did not know of the works the Lord wrote through him.

LAST WORDS & DEATH OF ST. NICHOLAS

𝕹icholas faithfully shepherded the flock in Myra for many years. As was written of Simon the High Priest in the 2nd century BC (Sirach 50), so it could be said of Nicholas:

> He was as the morning star in the midst
> of a cloud, and as the moon at the full; as the
> sun shining upon the temple of the Most High
> God...and as lilies by the rivers of waters...and
> as precious myrrh making all fragrant all his life.

Bishop Nicholas died on December 6, 343 AD. His last words were from Psalm 11, "In the Lord I put my trust!" At his burial the bishops of Lycia gathered with all the clergy and monastics and a countless multitude of people from all cities. His body was laid with honor in the cathedral church of the diocese of Myra.

Stories of the life and acts of Nicholas spread throughout Turkey into Greece and throughout the Roman Empire. Many legends of miracles arose regarding him, but it was the tradition of "secret gift-giving" on the anniversary of his death that became the most popular.

CLEMENT OF ALEXANDRIA, 215 AD

The earliest discussion of the date of the nativity is in the writings of Clement of Alexandria (c.150-215 AD), *Stromata (Miscellanies)*, Book 1, Chapter XXI.

POPE LIBERIUS, 354 AD

The tradition was that the Angel Gabriel appeared to Zacharaias, telling him his wife would become pregnant while he was in the Temple for the Day of Atonement, which would have been in September. His wife, Elizabeth, was six months pregnant with John the Baptist when Mary visited her, which would make the date of the Annunciation, when Gabriel appeared unto Mary and she conceived by the Holy Spirit, around March 25th. Nine months later would therefore be the day of Jesus' birth, December 25th.

In 354, just 40 years after Constantine ended the persecution of Christians, Pope Liberius led a successful effort to end the worship of the Roman Saturn, the "god of the unconquered sun." In order to celebrate the superiority of Christianity over paganism, Pope Liberius replaced the pagan day with the worship of the true Unconquered Son of God, Jesus Christ. The word "Christmas" comes from "Christ's Mass" or the "Mass of Christ," which means the celebration of the Christ, the Messiah, the Anointed One.

St. John Chrysostom, 386 AD

There Really is a Santa Claus

ST. JOHN CHRYSOSTOM, 386 AD

On December 20, 386 AD, St. John Chrysostom (347-407 AD) preached the first known Christmas sermon in the city of Antioch. It was titled "Homily on Christmas Morning."

EMPEROR JUSTINIAN, 430 AD

The Emperor Justinian (483-565) built a church in the year 430 AD, in Blacharnae, a suburb of Constantinople, and named it for Saint Nicholas.

BAPTISM OF CLOVIS, 496 AD

On Christmas Day, in the year 496 AD, Clovis (466-511), the King of the Franks, along with 3,000 of his warriors converted to Christianity and were baptized by Saint Remigius in Rheims, France. The name "Clovis" came to be pronounced "Louis," which was the name of 22 French Kings.

COUNCIL OF TOURS, 567 AD

The Council of Tours, in the year 567 AD, tried to reconcile the controversy between the Eastern Church and the Western Church. Christmas Day, December 25th, recognizing Christ's birth, was remembered in Western Europe as the holiest day of the season, and Epiphany,

VLADIMIR, 988 AD

January 6th, recognizing the visit of the wise men (and Jesus' baptism), was remembered in Eastern Europe.

Since no agreement could be reached as to which day was holier, the decision was made to have all 12 days between December 25th and January 6th "holy days," or as it was later pronounced "holidays." These became known as the "Twelve Days of Christmas."

CORONATION OF CHARLEMANGE, 800 AD

On Christmas Day, in 800 AD, Charlemagne (768-814), King of France, was knighted Emperor of the Holy Roman Empire by Pope Leo III.

CONVERSION OF VLADIMIR, 988 AD

In 988, Vladimir the Great (980-1015), the grand prince of Russia, converted to Christianity and traveled to the city of Constantinople, Turkey, to be baptized. While there, he heard of Saint Nicholas, or "Nikolai," and was so impressed that he chose him as the patron saint of all Russia, a nation covering one-sixth of the world.

The Primary Chronicle is a history of ancient Russia from 850 AD to 1110 AD, compiled in Kiev in 1113. It tells how in 986 AD, Prince Vladimir was visited by some Bulgar Muslims from Khwarezm, inviting him to adopt Islam.

Originally a pagan, Vladimir asked them to explain their religion:

They replied that they believed in Allah, and that Mohammed instructed them to practice circumcision, to eat no pork, to drink no wine, and after death, promised them complete fulfillment of their carnal desires.

"Mohammed," they asserted, "will give each man 70 fair women. He may choose one fair one, and upon that woman will Mohammed confer the charms of them all, and she shall be his wife.

"Mohammed promises that one may then satisfy every desire. But whoever is poor in this world will be no different in the next."

They also spoke other false things (which out of modesty may not be written down).

Vladimir listened to them, for he was fond of women and indulgence, regarding which he heard with pleasure. But circumcision and abstinence from pork and wine were disagreeable to him.

"Drinking," said he, "is the joy of the Russes. We cannot exist without that pleasure."

Prince Vladimir was also visited by Germans from the Latin Roman Catholic Church and Jewish Khazars. Finally Vladimir was visited by Greeks from the Eastern Orthodox Church, whose beautiful Hagia Sophia Cathedral in Constantinople was the largest and most ornate church in the world for over a thousand years.

After hearing an explanation of the Gospel, and learning that the New Testament had been written in Greek and that many cities mentioned in the New Testament were

There Really is a Santa Claus

located in the Byzantine Empire, Vladimir converted to Eastern Orthodox Christianity and ordered all pagan idols in Russia cast into the Dnieper River.

Vladimir also adopted the Eastern Orthodox Saint Nicholas as the Patron Saint of Russia. There was, perhaps, not a single city in Russia without a church named after Saint Nicholas.

SAINT STEPHEN CROWNED, 1000 AD

On Christmas Day, in the year 1000 AD, St. Stephen (died 1038) was crowned the apostolic King of Hungary.

MUSLIMS INVADE - ST. NICHOLAS' BONES, 1087 AD

In 1087, the Muslim Seljuk Turks staged a bloody invasion into Asia Minor (modern day Turkey,) killing Christians, turning Byzantine churches into mosques and desecrating the graves of Saints.

The Christians in this region, which included the seven churches mentioned in the Book of Revelation, were all but wiped out.

Concern arose for the remains of Saint Nicholas, the most famous saint in the Eastern Orthodox Church, as the Muslim practice was to destroy the graves of Christian Saints and give their bones to the dogs, as Mohammed instructed (Vol 2, Book 23, No. 414):

Bari, Italy

There Really is a Santa Claus

"Allah cursed the Jews and the Christians because they took the graves of their Prophets as places for praying," and "Do not leave an image without obliterating it, or a high grave without leveling it." (Hadith Sahih Muslim, 2115)

Islamic teaching is that not only should there be no images of Allah, the Hadith states there should be no images in art:

Abu'l-Hayyaj al-Asadi told that 'Ali (b. Abu Talib) said to him: Should I not send you on the same mission as Allah's Messenger (may peace be upon him) sent me? Do not leave an image without obliterating it, or a high grave without leveling it.

This hadith has been reported by Habib with the same clain of transmitters and he said: (Do not leave) a picture without obliterating it. (Hadith Book 4, No. 2115)

Just as the bones of St. Mark were smuggled out of Muslim controlled Egypt in 828 AD, by packing them under pork and shipping them to Venice, Italy, so a plan emerged to smuggle the remains of St. Nicholas to Italy in 1087 AD.

Certain merchants from **Bari, Italy**, a seaport in the kingdom of Naples situated on the Adriatic Gulf, sailed three ships to Myra, on the coast of Lycia. When no Muslims were around, they went to the church, about 3 miles inland, where St. Nicholas' remains were kept. They broke open the marble coffin and carried St. Nicholas' bones to their ships.

They landed on May 9, 1087, at Bari, and the archbishop oversaw the carrying of the sacred treasure to the Church of St. Stephen.

A basilica was begun in 1087, during the Italo-Norman domination of Apulia, in an area previously occupied by the Byzantine Catapan. Pope Urban II was present at the consecration of the crypt in 1089. The edifice was officially consecrated in 1197, in the presence of the Imperial Vicar, Bishop Conrad of Hildesheim.

May 9th is the day celebrated annually in the Russian Orthodox Church as the feast day of the "Translation of the Relics of Saint Nicholas from Myra to Bari."

The tomb of St. Nicholas of Bari became a famous location for pilgrimages. Italy, then France, and finally all Western Europe grew in their admiration of the life of Saint Nicholas. His feast day, December 6th, the anniversary of his death, was celebrated with the custom of "secret gift-giving" and many other imaginative traditions.

So popular has St. Nicholas become that over 250 churches in the United States, 400 churches in England, and over 1,200 worldwide have been dedicated in his honor.

Saint Nicholas' remains are still located in the Catedral de San Nicolás de Bari, (Basilica di San Nicola) in southern Italy.

On December 28, 2009, the Turkish newspaper, *Hurriyet Daily News,* reported that Muslims of Demre (Turkish name for Myra) were considering demanding the remains of St. Nicholas be returned for a tourist attraction:

> Culture and Tourism Minister Ertu'rul Günay told reporters in Antalya on Sunday that there were plans to demand the return of the bones of St. Nicholas.

A suggestion is that the bones of St. Nicholas should be returned to Turkey only after Muslims return Turkey to the Byzantine Christians.

VENI, VENI EMMANUEL, 1100 AD

In the 1100's was written the Latin Christmas hymn, Veni, Veni Emmanuel:

FRANCIS OF ASSISI & NATIVITY SCENE, 1223 AD

By 1223, so much attention was being given to gifts and gift-giving during the Christmas season, that Saint Francis of Assisi (1181-1226) was concerned that the emphasis on material things was overshadowing the spiritual things, diverting people's attention from Christ. ("Christmas" or "Christ's Mass," literally means the celebration of Christ.) In an effort to return to the reason for the season and bring the focus back to the simplicity of Jesus' birth, Francis created the first creche or nativity scene.

COLUMBUS, 1492 AD

When Christopher Columbus (1451-1506) discovered a port in Haiti on December 6, 1492, he named it in honor of Saint Nicholas, the "Patron Saint of Sailors."

BIBLICAL THEMES & ST. NICHOLAS

€ventually themes from the Bible began to be transitioned into legends and traditions of Saint Nicholas.

*Jesus will return at the end of the world riding a white horse to judge the living and the dead...

> Revelation 19:11-16 "And I saw heaven opened, and behold a white horse; and he that sat upon him was called Faithful and True, and in righteousness he doth judge...and his name is called The Word of God...And he hath on his vesture and on his thigh a name written, KING OF KINGS, AND LORD OF LORDS."

*The saints would return with him...

> 1 Thessalonians 4:14-17 "For if we believe that Jesus died and rose again, even so them also which sleep in Jesus will God bring with him...
> For the Lord himself shall descend from heaven with a shout, with the voice of the archangel, and with the trump of God: and the dead in Christ shall rise first: Then we which are alive and remain shall be caught up together with them in the clouds, to meet the Lord in the air."

There Really is a Santa Claus

*The saints and angels would also be riding white horses...

> Revelation 19:14 "And the armies which were in heaven followed him upon white horses, clothed in fine linen, white and clean."

The legend gradually transitioned into Saint Nicholas coming back once a year as sort of a mini pre-judgment day, to check up on whether children were being bad or good.

*Norway, Sweden, Finland, Denmark and northern Russia, had few horses, so the legend gradually transitioned into Saint Nicholas riding a reindeer.

*In heaven the "Lamb's Book of Life" has written in it the names of all believers:

> Revelation 21:27 "And there shall in no wise enter into it any thing that defileth, neither whatsoever worketh abomination, or maketh a lie: but they which are written in the Lamb's Book of Life."

> Revelation 3:5 "He that overcometh, the same shall be clothed in white raiment; and I will not blot out his name out of the Book of Life, but I will confess his name before my Father, and before his angels."

In heaven are also the "Books of Works":

Revelation 20:12 "And I saw the dead, small and great, stand before God; and the books were opened...and the dead were judged out of those things which were written in the books, according to their works."

Matthew 16:27 "For the Son of man shall come in the glory of his Father with his angels; and then he shall reward every man according to his works."

The angels, who were assumed to help keep the "Books of Works," gradually transitioned into elves helping to keep the book of the naughty and the nice.

*Jesus and the saints will come from heaven, the celestial city, the New Jerusalem...

Revelation 21:2-4 "I saw the Holy City, the new Jerusalem, coming down out of heaven from God, prepared as a bride beautifully dressed for her husband.

And I heard a loud voice from the throne saying, "Look! God's dwelling place is now among the people, and he will dwell with them.

They will be his people, and God himself will be with them and be their God. 'He will wipe every tear from their eyes. There will be no more death' or mourning or crying or pain, for the old order of things has passed away."

The New Jerusalem, the celestial city, gradually transitioned into the North Pole.

TRADITIONS

BELGIUM

In Belgium Saint Nicholas was thought to come from the Celestial City in heaven on his feast day, riding a white horse carrying a book in which the Guardian Angels had carefully recorded each child's deeds. He would then reward the good children with sweets and punish the wicked with switches, similar to when "the Lord himself shall descend from heaven" on a "white horse" to "reward every man according to his works."

GERMANY

In Germany, St. Nicholas is called "Weinachtsmann" and is said to visit homes on the eve of his feast day. He is accompanied by Krampus, an ugly, chain-rattling little devil who deals with children who have been naughty. The anticipation of this visit brought children an anxiety akin to the "Day of Judgment."

FRANCE

In France, Saint Nicholas is called "Piere Noel." Children would leave their slippers and wooden shoes on

Saint Nicholas, good holy man!
Put on the Tabard,* best you can,
Go, clad therewith, to Amsterdam,
From Amsterdam to Hispanje,
Where apples *bright* † of Oranje,
And likewise those *granate* ‡ surnam'd,
Roll through the streets, all free unclaim'd.
Saint Nicholas, my dear good friend!
To serve you ever was my end,
If you will, now, me something give,
I'll serve you ever while I live.

There Really is a Santa Claus

their doorsteps filled with oats to feed the camels of the three wise men. The next morning they discovered their kindness rewarded as their shoes were filled with sugared-plums.

ITALY

In Italy, St. Nicholas is called "Babbo Natale."

FINLAND

In Finland, St. Nicholas is called "Joulupukki."

SWEDEN

In Sweden, St. Nicholas is called "Tomten."

NORWAY

In Norway, St. Nicholas is called "Julnissen."

DENMARK

In Denmark, a superstitious tradition that continued from their pagan history was a Nisse. This was a small, gnome-like creature, referred to as an "elf" or "sprite" which lived in their house or barn. It had a long white beard, wore a red cap, and was given to mischief. It was customary for the family to leave out a plate of porridge on Christmas Eve

to appease the spirit so it would not cause mischief, similar to leaving a "treat" at Halloween so they would not get "tricked."

NETHERLANDS

In the Netherlands, Saint Nicholas is called "Sinterklaas." He arrives in Holland on a boat from Spain. Dressed in a bishop's robes and carrying a pastoral staff, he rides a white horse across the rooftops with his Moorish costumed helper, Zwarte Piet, checking on the children.

The good children received gifts, while the naughty children were threatened with being put in a gunny sack by Zwarte Piet and taken back to Spain where they would be sold into Muslim slavery. Often children would be brought to tears when reminded of St. Nicholas' imminent visit.

Muslims controlled Spain for 700 years, and millions of Europeans were captured from towns in Spain and Portugal, Greek Islands and Italian coasts and sold into Muslim harems, caravans or as galley slaves. In the 16th and 17th centuries, more Europeans were carried away south across the Mediterranean into the Muslim slavery of North Africa, than Africans, purchased at Muslim slave markets, who were carried west to the Americas.

Even one of the Pilgrim ships was captured by the Muslims in 1625. After living in the Netherlands for 12 years, the Pilgrims borrowed money from English "adventurers" to finance their voyage to Massachusetts in 1620. They paid back these adventurers with beaver skins and dried fish. It took nearly forty years to repay this debt, due in part to losses at sea, such as what happened in 1625.

There Really is a Santa Claus

Governor William Bradford recorded in his *History of the Plymouth Settlement 1608-1650* (rendered in Modern English by Harold Paget, 1909, chap. 6, pps. 165-167), that the Pilgrims had filled:

> Two fishing ships...with corfish...to bring home to England...and besides...some 800 lbs. of beaver, as well as other furs, to a good value from the plantation...
>
> They went joyfully home together and had such fine weather...till they were well within the England channel, almost in sight of Plymouth.
>
> But even there she was unhapply taken by a Turkish man-of-war and carried off to Saller [Morocco], where the captain and crew were made slaves...Thus all their hopes were dashed and the joyful news they meant to carry home was turned to heavy tidings...
>
> The friendly adventurers were so reduced by their losses last year, and now by the ship taken by the Turks...that all trade was dead.

Between 1606-1609, Muslim corsair pirates from Algeria captured 466 British and Scotish ships. Giles Milton wrote in White Gold: The Extraordinary Story of Thomas Pellow and North Africa's One Million European Slaves (UK: Hodder & Stoughton Ltd, 2004), that Muslim pirates raided England in 1625, even sailing up the Thames River.

Attacking the coast of Cornwall, they captured 60 villagers at Mount's Bay and 80 at Looe. Muslims took Lundy Island in Bristol Channel and raised the standard of Islam.

There Really is a Santa Claus

By the end of 1625, over 1,000 English subjects were sent to the slave markets of Sale, Morocco.

Between July 4-19, 1627, Algerian and Ottoman Muslim pirates, led by Murat Reis the Younger, raided Iceland, carrying into slavery an estimated 400 from the cities of Reykjavik, Austurland and Vestmannaeyjar. One captured girl, who had been made a slave concubine in Algeria, was rescued back by King Christian IV of Denmark.

On June 20, 1631, the entire village of Baltimore, Ireland was captured by Muslim pirates, led by Murat Reis the Younger. Only two ever returned. (see: Des Ekin's *The Stolen Village: Baltimore and the Barbary Pirates*, O'Brien Press, 2006). Thomas Osborne Davis wrote in his poem, "The Sack of Baltimore" (1895):

> The yell of 'Allah!'
> breaks above the shriek and roar;
> O'blessed God!
> the Algerine is lord of Baltimore.

Robert C. Davis' book, *Christian Slaves, Muslim Masters: White Slavery in the Mediterranean, the Barbary Coast and Italy 1500-1800* (Palgrave Macmillian, 2003), gives the record of Francis Knight, an Englishman who had been kidnapped and enslaved in Algiers, then made a slave on Algerian galleys for seven years:

> January the 16th day, in the year before nominated [1631]; I arrived in [Algiers,] that citie fatall to all Christians, and the butchery of mankind...my condolation is for the losse of many Christians, taken from their parents and countries, of all sorts and

sexes. Some in infancy, both by land and by sea, being forced to abuses (most incorrigible flagitions) not onely so, but bereaft of Christian religion, and means of grace and repentence.

How many thousands of the Nazarian nations have beene and are continually lost by that monster, what rational creature can be ignorant of?

Upon arrival in North Africa, infidel Christian slaves were jeered and pelted with stones by children as they were marched to the auction block. Men were often made galley slaves and women became servants or were paraded naked and sold as sex slaves. The whiter the skin, the higher the bid. Robert Davis described the end of the 17th century:

The Italian peninsula had by then been prey to the Barbary corsairs for two centuries or more, and its coastal populations had largely withdrawn into walled hilltop villages or larger towns like Rimini, abandoning miles of once populous shoreline.

The Calabrian coast of Italy suffered: 700 captured in 1636; 1,000 in 1639; and 4,000 in 1644. Some coastal areas lost their entire child-bearing population. Muslims corsair raiders desecrated churches and stole church bells to silence the distinctive sound of Christianity.

By 1640, hundreds of English ships and over 3,000 Britishsubjects were enslaved in Algiers and 1,500 in Tunis.

In three centuries, over a million Europeans were enslaved by Muslim Barbary Pirates.

There Really is a Santa Claus

Giles Milton wrote of Thomas Pellow, born in an English fishing village in 1704. At the age of 11, Pellow was on board his uncle's ship when it was captured by Muslim Barbary Pirates. He became property of Sultan Moulay Ismail, and, along with 25,000 other white slaves, was put to work building the Sultan's grand palace in Meknes, called the "Versailles of Morocco."

Sultan Ismail ordered soldiers to push Christian slaves off a high wall they were building because they did not synchronize their hammer strokes. He beat his slaves "in the cruelest manner imaginable, to try if they were hard" and murdered some for "hiding pieces of bread." He had 500 wives, mostly captured European women, who bore him a record 1,042 children.

An account of Sultan Moulay Ismail, titled *A Journey to Mequinez (Meknes)*, written by John Windus (London, 1825), stated:

> His trembling court assemble, which consists of...blacks, whites, tawnies and his favourite Jews, all barefooted...
>
> He is...known by his very looks...and sometimes the colour of the habit that he wears, yellow being observed to be his killing colour; from all of which they calculate whether they may hope to live twenty-four hours longer..."
>
> When he goes out of town...he will be attended by fifteen or twenty thousand blacks on horseback, with whom he now and then diverts himself at (by throwing) the lance...

His travelling utensils are two or three guns, a sword or two, and two lances, because one broke once while he was murdering;

His boys carry short Brazil sticks, knotted cords for whipping, a change of clothes to shift when bloody, and a hatchet, two of which he took in a Portuguese ship, and the first time they were bought to him, killed a man without any provocation, to try if they were good.

Witnessing tortures, beheadings and forced conversions to Islam, Thomas Pellow escaped after 23 years. A distant relative, Sir Edward Pellew, led the British fleet to bombard Algiers in 1816, freeing thousands of slaves.

In 1228, the Catholic Order of Trinitarians, also called Mathurins, was founded by St. John of Math, a doctor of the University of Paris. The sole purpose of the Order, stated in its Latin title "Ordo S. Trinitatis et de Redemptione Captivorum," was to raise money from across Europe to ransom thousands of Christian prisoners and slaves from the Mussulmen (Muslims).

In 1230, the Catholic Order of Mercedarians was organized in Spain for the same purpose, ransoming Christian captives from the Moors (Muslims). The head of the Order had the title "Ransomer."

MARTIN LUTHER & KRIS KRINGLE, 1517 AD

When the Reformation began in Germany, 1517, Martin Luther (1483-1546) ended all praying to or honoring

of saints, including Saint Nicholas, believing that Christ alone should be the focus of attention.

People liked the gift-giving, so Martin Luther sought to refocus the people's thoughts on the Christ Child, which in old German was pronounced "Kris Kindl" (Christkindl), later pronounced "Kris Kringle." He taught Christ was the giver of all gifts and our gift-giving should be in remembrance of the great gifts Christ gave us.

HENRY VIII & FATHER CHRISTMAS, 1534 AD

𝕴n 1534, King Henry VIII (1491-1547) was frustrated because he was unable to produce a male heir to the throne through his first wife, Catherine of Aragon, daughter of King Ferdinand and Queen Isabella of Spain. He wanted a divorce so he could marry another, but this was against the Church. King Henry VIII then broke the English church away from Rome, and along with this action, ended all honoring of saints, including Saint Nicholas.

King Henry VIII, like Martin Luther, recognized the importance people placed on Christmas traditions, but instead of bringing the focus back to the "Christ Child," Henry VIII introduced a character known as "Father Christmas," which was a throwback to "Saturn," the Roman god of plenty. He was pictured as a large man clothed in deep green or scarlet robes lined with fur, bringing peace, joy, good food, wine and revelry, similar to the "spirit of Christmas present" in Charles Dickens` *A Christmas Carol*. At this time of year, the ancient Romans celebrated "Saturnalia," honoring the pagan deity with a season of merriment, feasting, gift-giving and mending of

relationships. Since England no longer kept Saint Nicholas's feast day on December 6th, they moved their "Father Christmas" celebration to December 25th to coincide with Christmas Day.

During Henry VIII's reign, and up to the English Civil War in 1642 when the Puritans took over, Christmas became more of a party time in England, with carousing and holiday drinking. This is similar to what happened with Mardi Gras, which originally was a religious day before Lent when Christians would fast 40 days before Easter, yet it has devolved into a lewd party in New Orleans.

WASSAILING

"Wassailing" was the practice of pouring wassail punch (a mixture of ale, wine, spices and toasted apples) on their trees, fields, beehives, in an attempt to bring luck for the next year's harvests. Washington Irving wrote of wassailing in his *Old Christmas,* 1820:

> The Wassail Bowl was sometimes composed of ale instead of wine; with nutmeg, sugar, toast, ginger, and roasted crabs; in this way the nut-brown beverage is still prepared in some old families, and round the hearths of substantial farmers at Christmas. It is also called Lambs' Wool, and is celebrated by Herrick in his "Twelfth Night:"
> "Next crowne the bowle full
> With gentle Lambs' Wool,
> Add sugar, nutmeg, and ginger,

With store of ale too;
And thus ye must doe
To make the Wassaile a swinger."

The traditionary customs of golden-hearted antiquity, its feudal hospitalities, and lordly wassailings, have passed away with the baronial castles and stately manor-houses...

The service was followed by a Christmas carol, which Mr. Bracebridge himself had constructed from a poem of his favourite author, Herrick; and it had been adapted to an old church melody by Master Simon...Worthy Squire delivered one stanza: his eyes glistening, and his voice rambling out of all the bounds of time and tune:

"'Tis thou that crown'st my glittering hearth
With guiltlesse mirth,
And giv'st me wassaile bowles to drink,
Spiced to the brink:
Lord, 'tis Thy plenty-dropping hand,
That soiles my land;
And giv'st me for my bushell sowne,
Twice ten for one."

...The butler brought in a huge silver vessel of rare and curious workmanship, which he placed before the Squire. Its appearance was hailed with acclamation; being the Wassail Bowl, so renowned in Christmas festivity. The contents had been prepared by the Squire himself; for it was a

beverage in the skilful mixture of which he particularly prided himself...It was a potation, indeed, that might well make the heart of a toper leap within him; being composed of the richest and raciest wines, highly spiced and sweetened, with roasted apples bobbing about the surface...

There was much laughing and rallying, as the honest emblem of Christmas joviality circulated, and was kissed rather coyly by the ladies. When it reached Master Simon he raised it in both hands, and with the air of a boon companion struck up an old Wassail chanson:

> The browne bowle,
> The merry browne bowle,
> As it goes round about-a,
> Fill
> Still,
> Let the world say what it will,
> And drink your fill all out-a.
>
> The deep canne,
> The merry deep canne,
> As thou dost freely quaff-a,
> Sing,
> Fling,
> Be as merry as a king,
> And sound a lusty laugh-a.*
> *(From "Poor Robin's Almanack.")

...I found the tide of wine and wassail fast gaining on the dry land of sober judgment. The company grew merrier and louder as their jokes grew duller. Master Simon was in as chirping a humour as a grasshopper filled with dew; his old songs grew of a warmer complexion, and he began to talk maudlin about the widow.

He even gave a long song about the wooing of a widow, which he informed me he had gathered from an excellent black-letter work, entitled "Cupid's Solicitor for Love," containing store of good advice for bachelors, and which he promised to lend me. The first verse was to this effect:

"He that will woo a widow must not dally,
He must make hay while the sun doth shine;
He must not stand with her, Shall I, Shall I?
But boldly say, Widow, thou must be mine."

...There was a quaintness, too, mingled with all this revelry that gave it a peculiar zest; it was suited to the time and place; and as the old Manor House almost reeled with mirth and wassail, it seemed echoing back the joviality of long-departed years...

...The custom of drinking out of the same cup gave place to each having his cup. When the steward came to the doore with the Wassel, he was to cry three times, Wassel, Wassel, Wassel, and then the chappel

(chaplain) was to answer with a song.—
Archaeologia.

> Here we come a wassailing
> Among the leaves so green,
> Here we come a wandering
> So fair to be seen. (Chorus)
>
> Love and joy come to you,
> And to you your wassail too,
> And God bless you and send you
> a happy New Year.
> And God send you a happy New Year.
>
> Our wassail cup is made
> Of the rosemary tree,
> And so is your beer
> Of the best barley. (Chorus)
>
> We are not daily beggars
> That beg from door to door,
> But we are neighbours' children
> Whom you have seen before. (Chorus)
>
> Good Master and good Mistress,
> As you sit by the fire,
> Pray think of us poor children
> Are wandering in the mire. (Chorus)
>
> We have a little purse
> Made of ratching leather skin;
> We want some of your small change
> To line it well within. (Chorus)

Call up the Butler of this house,
Put on his golden ring;
Let him bring us a glass of beer,
And the better we shall sing. (Chorus)

Bring us out a table,
And spread it with a cloth;
Bring us out a mouldy cheese,
And some of your Christmas loaf. (Chorus)

God bless the Master of this house,
Likewise the Mistress too;
And all the little children
That round the table go. (Chorus)

CALVINIST REFORMERS, 1552 AD

𝕴n response the less biblical holiday traditions which existed during the time of Henry VIII, reformers sought to return the focus to the holiday's spiritual origins.

Calvinist reformer John Knox (1514-1572) brought the Protestant Reformation to Scotland in 1552, and Christmas celebrations ended. It was not until the invention of the television that they were reintroduced in the 1950's.

PILGRIMS, 1620 AD

𝕴n 1620, the Pilgrims sailed to Massachusetts. The captain of the Mayflower, Master Christopher Jones (1570-1622), wrote in his ship's log, December 25, 1620:

There Really is a Santa Claus

At anchor in Plymouth harbor, Christmas Day, but not observed by these colonists, they being opposed to all saints' days, etc....

A large party went ashore this morning to fell timber and begin building. They began to erect the first house about twenty feet square for their common use, to receive them and their goods.

William Bradford (1590-1657) wrote in *Of Plymouth Plantation*, that writing of the year 1621:

Herewith I shall end this year – except to recall one more incident, rather amusing than serious.

On Christmas Day the Governor called the people out to work as usual; but most of the new company excused themselves, and said it went against their consciences to work on that day. So the Governor told them, if they made it a matter of conscience, he would spare them till they were better informed.

So he went with the rest, and left them; but on returning from work at noon he found them at play in the street, some pitching the bar, some at stool-ball, and such like sports. So he went to them and took away their games, and told them that it was against his conscience that they should play and others work.

There Really is a Santa Claus

If they made the keeping of the day a matter of devotion, let them remain in their houses; but there should be no gaming and revelling in the streets.

Beginning in 1629, Puritans came to the shores of America. They did not celebrate Christmas, the Feast Day of Saint Nicholas or Henry VIII's "Father Christmas." They considered each day as belonging to the Lord and the weekly Sabbath was their special time of celebration.

PURITANS

In 1659, the Puritans of New England passed a law:

Whosoever shall be found observing any such day as Christmas and the like, either by forbearing labor, feasting, or any other way upon such account as aforesaid, every such person so shall pay for each offense five shillings as a fine to the country.

Puritan leader, Rev. Cotton Mather (1663-1728), told his congregation, December 25, 1712:

Can you in your Conscience think, that our Holy Saviour is honoured, by Mad Mirth, by long Eating, by hard Drinking, by lewd Gaming, by rude Revelling; by a Mass fit for none but a Saturn or a Bacchus, or the Night of a Mahometan Ramadam? You cannot possibly think so!

A Multitude of the Heavenly Host was heard Praising of God. But shall it be said, That at the Birth of our Saviour for which we owe as high Praises to God as they can do, we take the Time to Please the Hellish Legions, and to do Actions that have much more of Hell than of Heaven in them?

DUTCH SETTLE NEW AMSTERDAM, 1623 AD

Though Puritan colonists did not celebrate Christmas, other Protestants, such as the Dutch, did.

In 1623, Dutch immigrants settled New Amsterdam, which existed as a Dutch colony until 1664, when the British took control and turned the settlement into New York. Dutch settlers brought to the new world their Christmas traditions. They considered Saint Nicholas as the "Patron Saint" of New Amsterdam. The Dutch pronunciation of Saint Nicholas was "Sant Nicklaus," or "Sinter Klaas," or "Santa Claus."

In *Diedrich Knickerbocker's A History of New York from the Beginning of the New World to the End of the Dutch Dynasty,* 1809, Washington Irving wrote:

> Finally, that [Dutch citizens of New Amsterdam] should have all the benefits of free trade, and should not be required to acknowledge any other saint in the calendar than St. Nicholas, who should thenceforward, as before, be considered the tutelar saint of the city...

Dutch Reformed St. Nicholas Church, 1628 AD

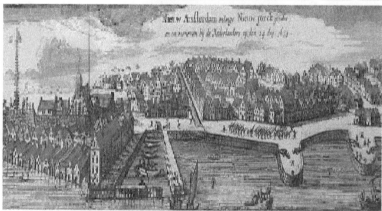

There Really is a Santa Claus

DUTCH REFORMED
ST. NICHOLAS CHURCH, 1628 AD

𝕴n *Diedrich Knickerbocker's A History of New York from the Beginning of the New World to the End of the Dutch Dynasty*, 1809, Washington Irving wrote of the Dutch settlers of New Amsterdam building a chapel, which they named for St. Nicholas:

> The earliest measures of this infant settlement, inasmuch as it shows the piety of our forefathers, and that, like good Christians, they were always ready to serve God, after they had first served themselves.
>
> Thus, having quietly settled themselves down, and provided for their own comfort, they bethought themselves of testifying their gratitude to the great and good **St. Nicholas**, for his protecting care in guiding them to this delectable abode.
>
> To this end they built a fair and goodly chapel within the fort, which they consecrated to his name; whereupon he immediately took the town of New Amsterdam under his peculiar patronage, and he has even since been, and I devoutly hope will ever be, the tutelar saint of this excellent city...
>
> I am moreover told that there is a little legendary book somewhere extant, written in Low Dutch, which says that the image of this renowned **saint**, which whilom graced the

bow-sprit of the Goede Vrouw, was elevated in front of this chapel...

He attended public service at the great church of **St. Nicholas**, like a true and pious governor...

...casting many a wistful look to the weathercock on the church of **St. Nicholas**...

NEW YORK'S DUTCH REFORMED ST. NICHOLAS CATHEDRAL

In an article on New York's Dutch Reformed Cathedral, Andrew Cusack wrote on St. Nicholas Day, December 6, 2008:

> The Collegiate Reformed Protestant Dutch Church of **Saint Nicholas**, on the corner of 48th Street & 5th Avenue, was for many years regarded as the most eminent Protestant church in New York...It is the oldest corporate body in what is now the United States, having been founded at the bottom of Manhattan in 1628...
>
> The first regular Calvinist services were held in the loft of a grist-mill not long after the foundation of New Amsterdam in 1624...
>
> In 1633, Dominie Everardus Bogardus arrived from the Netherlands and built a small wooden church on Broad Street between

Bridge and Pearl streets (across from where Fraunces Tavern now stands).

This was replaced by the stone church of **St. Nicholas** built inside Fort Amsterdam in 1642 (destroyed by fire in 1741).

In 1693, the Dutch congregation moved to a peach orchard on Garden Street (now Exchange Place) where they built a church "by far the most substantial and the finest yet built in Manhattan." The coats of arms of the church elders (and perhaps of other prominent families) were burnt into the glass windows by Gerardus Duycknick (father of the artist of the same name), and heraldic paintings may have decorate the walls as well.

A year later, the members of the congregation sent silver coins to Amsterdam for the casting of a baptismal bowl which was used well into the late 19th century...

The Dutch Church...received its royal charter from William & Mary in 1696...

In 1729, the Collegiate Reformed Protestant Dutch Church erected a second congregation on Nassau Street between Cedar and Crown streets (Crown was renamed Liberty Street after New York became an independent republic in 1783). The bell of the Middle Dutch Church was donated by Col. Abraham de Peyster.

North Dutch Church followed in 1769, and Middle Church moved to Lafayette Place in 1844 after their old church was

New Yorks' Dutch Reformed St. Nicholas Cathdral

There Really is a Santa Claus

leased to the federal government for use as a post office because of its spaciousness. (Supposedly the king's army had temporarily converted the building into a riding school for the Dragoons during the Revolution). The de Peyster bell was moved from Middle to **St. Nicholas** after it was dedicated in 1872.

The land on which the Church of **St. Nicholas** stood was purchased from Columbia University in 1857, but it was many years before construction commenced. A lecture room opened for worship services on Christmas Day in 1866, and the cornerstone of the church was finally laid in July 1869. **St. Nicholas** was the largest of the Collegiate churches and its location on 5th Avenue attracted many of the well-to-do families of the neighborhood, both of Dutch ancestry and otherwise.

(In fact, a letter to the editor of *The New York Times* was published in May 1896 complaining that, while "there was nothing spared" in the celebrations of the 200th anniversary of the royal charter, "none of the speakers of that evening was in a direct line a descendant from Holland, but rather from France and other foreign countries").

The church was completed in a lively gothic style in a humble Newark sandstone, and with a playful steeple of exaggerated size. While the presbyterian nature of its Reformed Calvinist polity allows no bishops,

because of its scale, social prominence, and location, **St. Nicholas** was often thought of as "the Protestant Cathedral of New York."

Regrettably, financial mismanagement forced the Church of St. Nicholas to close its doors in 1947 and the Dutch cathedral of New York was demolished in 1949. Just as the independence of India in 1947 presaged the collapse of the British Empire throughout the remainder of the 20th century, so did the destruction of **Saint Nicholas** presage the dissolution of the old order in New York. An office building for Sinclair Oil, rather bland yet relatively inoffensive, was constructed in its place and remains there today.

WASHINGTON IRVING & A HISTORY OF NEW YORK, 1809 AD

𝖂ashington Irving (1783-1859) was an entertaining early American writer who often mixed amusing legends and superstitions in with his humorous renditions of history. Similar to American folklore "tale tales" of the giant lumberjack "Paul Bunyan" and his Blue Ox, "Babe," Washington Irving's stories included *Rip Van Winkle* and *Legend of Sleepy Hollow*.

In 1809, Washington Irving wrote *Diedrich Knickerbocker's A History of New York from the Beginning of the New World to the End of the Dutch Dynasty*, a book which stayed in print over 20 years. In it, he made numerous delightful references to **St. Nicholas**:

So we are told, in the sylvan days of New Amsterdam, the good **St. Nicholas** would often make his appearance in his beloved city, of a holiday afternoon, riding jollily among the treetops, or over the roofs of houses, now and then drawing forth magnificent presents from his breeches pockets, and dropping them down the chimneys of his favorites...

He never shows us the light of his countenance, nor ever visits us, save one night in the year; when he rattles down the chimneys of the descendants of the patriarchs, confining his presents merely to the children...

The good **St. Nicholas** came riding over the tops of the trees, in that self-same wagon wherein he brings his yearly presents to children. And he descended hard...And he lit his pipe by the fire...

And when **St. Nicholas** had smoked his pipe he twisted it in his hatband, and laying his finger beside his nose, gave...a very significant look, then mounting his wagon, he returned over the treetops and disappeared...

The significant sign of **St. Nicholas**, laying his finger beside his nose and winking hard with one eye...

Washington Irving described how the Dutch settlers had exchanged St. Nicholas' bishop's robes, staff and mitered hat for a typical Dutch outfit:

There Really is a Santa Claus

A goodly image of **St. Nicholas**, equipped with a low, broad-brimmed hat, a huge pair of Flemish trunk hose, and a pipe...

The good **St. Nicholas**, who had appeared to him in a dream the night before, and whom he had known by his broad hat, his long pipe...

Swore by the pipe of **St. Nicholas**...

The Dutch settlers continued the tradition of hanging stockings by the fireplace:

At this early period was instituted that pious ceremony, still religiously observed in all our ancient families of the right breed, of hanging up a stocking in the chimney on **St. Nicholas Eve**; which stocking is always found in the morning miraculously filled; for the good **St. Nicholas** has ever been a great giver of gifts, particularly to children...

Nor was the day of **St. Nicholas** suffered to pass by without making presents, hanging the stocking in the chimney, and complying with all its other ceremonies...

Washington Irving mentioned "the festival of **St. Nicholas**" in his description of life in New Amsterdam, which was a Dutch settlement from 1624 to when the British took over in 1664:

The province of the New Netherlands...possessed a sweet tranquility that wealth could never purchase. There were neither public commotions, nor private quarrels...I am told every dutiful wife throughout New Amsterdam made a point of enriching her husband with at least one child a year...

In those good days of simplicity and sunshine, a passion for cleanliness was the leading principle in domestic economy, and the universal test of an able housewife—a character which formed the utmost ambition of our unenlightened grandmothers.

The front door was never opened except on marriages, funerals, new year's days, the festival of **St. Nicholas**, or some such great occasion.

SAINT NICHOLAS CHURCH & "SILENT NIGHT," 1818 AD

At **St. Nicholas** Church in Oberndorf bei Salzburg, Austria, December 24, 1818, the song, Silent Night was first performed.

CLEMENT MOORE & "A VISIT FROM ST. NICHOLAS," 1823 AD

The next major contributor to **Saint Nicholas'** new image was Reverend Clement Clarke Moore, Ph.D., (1779-

1863) a young Episcopal priest and Hebrew professor at a theological seminary. The father of six children, Rev. Clement Moore wrote an imaginative poem for his family in 1823 entitled "**A Visit from St. Nicholas**." Being the first identifiable author to mention Saint Nicholas in a sled being pulled by reindeer, Moore gave his amusing description of the saintly Bishop of Myra:

'TWAS the night before Christmas,
when all through the house
Not a creature was stirring,
not even a mouse;

The stockings were hung
by the chimney with care,
In hopes that **St. Nicholas**
soon would be there;

The children were nestled
all snug in their beds,
While visions of sugar-plums
danced in their heads;

And mamma in her 'kerchief,
and I in my cap,
Had just settled our brains
for a long winter's nap,

When out on the lawn
there arose such a clatter,
I sprang from the bed
to see what was the matter.

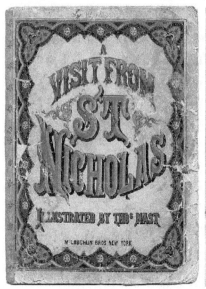

There Really is a Santa Claus

Away to the window
I flew like a flash,
Tore open the shutters
and threw up the sash.

The moon on the breast
of the new-fallen snow
Gave the lustre of mid-day
to objects below,

When, what to my wondering
eyes should appear,
But a miniature sleigh,
and eight tiny reindeer,

With a little old driver,
so lively and quick,
I knew in a moment
it must be **St. Nick.**

More rapid than eagles
his coursers they came,
And he whistled, and shouted,
and called them by name;

"Now, Dasher! now, Dancer!
now, Prancer and Vixen!
On, Comet! on, Cupid!
on, Donder and Blitzen!

To the top of the porch!
to the top of the wall!
Now dash away! dash away!
dash away all!"

As dry leaves that before
the wild hurricane fly,
When they meet with an obstacle,
mount to the sky;

So up to the house-top
the coursers they flew,
With the sleigh full of Toys,
and **St. Nicholas** too.

And then, in a twinkling,
I heard on the roof
The prancing and pawing
of each little hoof.

As I drew in my head,
and was turning around,
Down the chimney **St. Nicholas**
came with a bound.

He was dressed all in fur,
from his head to his foot,
And his clothes were all tarnished
with ashes and soot;

A bundle of Toys
he had flung on his back,
And he looked like a pedler
just opening his pack.

His eyes—how they twinkled!
his dimples how merry!
His cheeks were like roses,
his nose like a cherry!

His droll little mouth
was drawn up like a bow
And the beard of his chin
was as white as the snow;

The stump of a pipe
he held tight in his teeth,
And the smoke it encircled
his head like a wreath;

He had a broad face
and a little round belly,
That shook when he laughed,
like a bowlful of jelly.

He was chubby and plump,
a right jolly old elf,
And I laughed when I saw him,
in spite of myself;

A wink of his eye
and a twist of his head,
Soon gave me to know
I had nothing to dread;

He spoke not a word,
but went straight to his work,
And filled all the stockings;
then turned with a jerk,

And laying his finger
aside of his nose,
And giving a nod,
up the chimney he rose;

He sprang to his sleigh,
to his team gave a whistle,
And away they all flew
like the down of a thistle,

But I heard him exclaim,
ere he drove out of sight,
"Happy Christmas to all,
and to all a good-night."

THOMAS NAST – CIVIL WAR ILLUSTRATOR, 1862 AD

Thomas Nast (1840-1902) was the great American political cartoonist responsible for creating the Democratic "Mule" and the Republican "Elephant." In 1862, he sketched his first drawings of Santa Claus for *Harper's Weekly Magazine*. By this time, the name "**Saint Nicholas**" had evolved from the Dutch "**Sant Niklass**" to "**Sinter Klaas**" to "**Santa Claus**."

Over the next 22 years, Thomas Nast would publish over thirty such cartoons, depicting **Santa Claus** as a type of Bavarian Father Christmas, jolly, plump, with gnome-like features and an infectious outgoing personality.

He carried a long telescope, a record book, and for the first time had a "North Pole" sign behind him, which was a demoralizing moment for the South during the Civil War!

All of Thomas Nast's drawings were in black and white, until he was asked by McLoughlin Brothers publishing to do a final series of cartoons in color. This was the first time **Santa Claus** had a red suit with white fur trim.

HADDON SUNDBLOM & COCA-COLA, 1930 AD

The final adaptation of **St. Nicholas** to the present **Santa Claus** occurred in the 1930's, when Chicago artist Haddon Sundblom (1899-1976), who was famous his design of the Quaker Oats Man. Haddon Sundblom was contracted by the Coca-Cola Company to illustrate **Santa Claus** for their advertising campaign, which he did for 33 years. Haddon Sundblom portrayed **Santa Claus** as more warm and human, with blue eyes, ruby red lips and a ruddy complexion.

This new Santa took America by storm, as the invention of television and the techniques of mass-media marketing displayed this image in magazines, products, store displays, stationary and Christmas decorations.

IMAGINATION

Theologians define 5 qualities that God alone possesses:
Omniscience (all knowing);
Omnipresence (everywhere at the same time);
Omnipotent (all powerful);
Eternal (never dies);
Immutable (unchanging, perfect).

These five qualities, along with God being the giver of rewards and judgments, were imaginatively superimposed on **Santa Claus**, as demonstrated in the popular song "**Santa Claus is Coming to Town**":

Oh you better watch out
You better not cry,
You better watch out
I'm telling you why
Santa Claus is coming to town
He sees you when you're sleeping
He knows when you're awake
He knows if you've been bad or good
So be good for goodness sake.

In recent history, imaginative stories, songs and traditions were added on to the Christmas celebration:

"Frosty the Snowman"
"Rudolph the Red-nosed Reindeer"
"The Grinch that Stole Christmas"
"Jingle Bells"
"I'm Dreaming of a White Christmas"
"Silver Bells"
"Santa Baby"
"Chestnuts Roasting on an Open Fire."

REMEMBERING ST. NICHOLAS

To enter into the Christmas spirit, it is necessary to remember the Christmas story of the birth of Christ.

One should also remember that there really was a **Santa Claus**, the godly **Saint Nicholas**, who was willing to be imprisoned for his sincere Christian faith under Emperor Diocletian, who preached against pagan immorality of Diana worship, who stood for the Bible and doctrinal purity at the Council of Nicea, and who generously helped the poor, anonymously, so that the glory would go to God.

❦

CHRISTMAS TRADITIONS & HISTORY

IN THE YEAR 215 AD DATE OF NATIVITY

Clement of Alexandria (c.150-215 AD) was the first to discuss the possible dates of Jesus' nativity, though he offers little explanation:

> And there are those who have determined not only the year of our Lord's birth, but also the day; and they say that it took place in the twenty-eighth year of Augustus, and in the twenty-fifth day of Pachon. (Clement of Alexandria, *Stromata-Miscellanies*, Book 1, Chapter XXI).

> And our Lord was born in the twenty-eighth year, when first the census was ordered to be taken in the reign of Augustus. (Clement of Alexandria, *Stromata-Miscellanies*, Book 1, Chapter XXI).

> Others say that...He was born on the twenty-fourth or twenty-fifth of Pharmuthi. (Clement of Alexandria, *Stromata-Miscellanies)*, Book 1, Chapter XXI).

January 6th, the traditional date of Jesus' baptism, was sometimes observed, as Clement mentioned:

> And the followers of Basilides hold the day of his baptism as a festival, spending the night before in readings. And they say that it was the fifteenth year of Tiberius Caesar, the fifteenth day of the month Tubi; and some that it was the eleventh of the same month. (Clement of Alexandria, *Stromata-Miscellanies*, Book 1, Chapter 21).

IN THE YEAR 354 AD
CHRISTMAS DAY

𝕿he Christmas Holiday has a fascinating history. Scholars are undecided as to the exact date of Christ's birth, whether in the winter, spring or fall and whether it was between 4 BC or 1 AD. Without discounting efforts to discern the exact date of Christ's birth, the important fact is that he was born. In 354, Pope Liberius set December 25th at the date of Christmas, "Christ's Mass," which means the celebration of the Christ, the Messiah, the Anointed One.

IN THE YEAR 386 AD
THE FIRST CHRISTMAS SERMON

𝕾t. John Chrysostom (347-407 AD), preached the first known Christmas sermon on December 20, 386 AD, in the city of Antioch. It was titled "Homily on Christmas Morning":

Behold a new and wondrous mystery. My ears resound to the Shepherd's song, piping no soft melody, but chanting full forth a heavenly hymn. The Angels sing. The Archangels blend their voice in harmony. The Cherubim hymn their joyful praise. The Seraphim exalt His glory.

All join to praise this holy feast, beholding the Godhead here on earth, and man in heaven. He Who is above, now for our redemption dwells here below; and he that was lowly is by divine mercy raised.

Bethlehem this day resembles heaven; hearing from the stars the singing of angelic voices; and in place of the sun, enfolds within itself on every side, the Sun of justice. And ask not how: for where God wills, the order of nature yields. For He willed; He had the power; He descended; He redeemed; all things yielded in obedience to God.

This day He Who is, is Born; and He Who is, becomes what He was not. For when He was God, He became man; yet not departing from the Godhead that is His. Nor yet by any loss of divinity became He man, nor through increase became He God from man; but being the Word He became flesh, His nature, because of impassability, remaining unchanged.

And so the kings have come, and they have seen the heavenly King that has come upon the earth, not bringing with Him Angels, nor Archangels, nor Thrones, nor Dominations, nor Powers, nor Principalities, but, treading a new and solitary path, He has come forth from a spotless womb.

Since this heavenly birth cannot be described, neither does His coming amongst us in these days permit of too curious scrutiny. Though I know that a Virgin this day gave birth, and I believe that God was begotten before all time, yet the manner of this generation I have learned to venerate in silence and I accept that this is not to be probed too curiously with wordy speech.

For with God we look not for the order of nature, but rest our faith in the power of Him who works.

What shall I say to you; what shall I tell you? I behold a Mother who has brought forth; I see a Child come to this light by birth. The manner of His conception I cannot comprehend.

Nature here rested, while the Will of God labored. O ineffable grace! The Only Begotten, Who is before all ages, Who cannot be touched or be perceived, Who is simple, without body, has now put on my body, that is visible and liable to corruption. For what reason? That coming amongst us he may teach us, and teaching, lead us by the hand to the things that men cannot see.

For since men believe that the eyes are more trustworthy than the ears, they doubt of that which they do not see, and so He has deigned to show Himself in bodily presence, that He may remove all doubt.

Christ, finding the holy body and soul of the Virgin, builds for Himself a living temple, and as He had willed, formed there a man from the Virgin; and, putting Him on, this day came forth; unashamed of the lowliness of our nature.

For it was to Him no lowering to put on what He Himself had made. Let that handiwork be forever glorified, which became the cloak of its own Creator. For as in the first creation of flesh, man could not be made before the clay had come into His hand, so neither could this corruptible body be glorified, until it had first become the garment of its Maker.

What shall I say! And how shall I describe this Birth to you? For this wonder fills me with astonishment. The Ancient of days has become an infant. He Who sits upon the sublime and heavenly Throne, now lies in a manger. And He Who cannot be touched, Who is simple, without complexity, and incorporeal, now lies subject to the hands of men. He Who has broken the bonds of sinners, is now bound by an infants bands. But He has decreed that ignominy shall become honor, infamy be clothed with glory, and total humiliation the measure of His Goodness.

For this He assumed my body, that I may become capable of His Word; taking my flesh, He gives me His spirit; and so He bestowing and I receiving, He prepares for me the treasure of Life. He takes my flesh, to sanctify me; He gives me His Spirit, that He may save me.

Come, then, let us observe the Feast. Truly wondrous is the whole chronicle of the Nativity. For this day the ancient slavery is ended, the devil confounded, the demons take to flight, the power of death is broken, paradise is unlocked, the curse is taken away, sin is removed from us, error driven out, truth has been brought back, the speech of kindliness diffused, and spreads on every side, a heavenly way of life has been inplanted on the earth, angels communicate with men without fear, and men now hold speech with angels.

Why is this? Because God is now on earth, and man in heaven; on every side all things commingle. He became Flesh. He did not become God. He was God. Wherefore He became flesh, so that He Whom heaven did not contain, a manger would this day receive. He was placed in a manger, so that He, by whom all things are nourished, may receive an infant's food from His Virgin Mother. So, the Father of all ages, as an infant at the breast, nestles in the virginal arms, that the Magi may more easily see Him. Since this day the Magi too have come, and made a beginning of withstanding tyranny; and the heavens give glory, as the Lord is revealed by a star.

To Him, then, Who out of confusion has wrought a clear path, to Christ, to the Father, and to the Holy Ghost, we offer all praise, now and for ever. Amen.

IN THE YEAR 496 AD
KING CLOVIS' BAPTISM

In 496, Clovis (466-511), the King of France, along with 3,000 of his warriors converted to Christianity and were baptized on Christmas Day in Rheims, France.

IN THE YEAR 567 AD
COUNCIL OF TOURS

In 567, at the Council of Tours, the church tried to reconcile the celebration of Christmas Day-the feast of Christ's birth, as remembered in western Europe on December 25th, and the celebration of Epiphany-the feast of the visit of the wise men (and Jesus' baptism), as remembered in eastern Europe on January 6th.

Since no agreement could be reached on a specific date, the decision was made to have all 12 days between December 25th and January 6th "holy days," or as it was later pronounced "holidays." These became known as the "Twelve Days of Christmas."

IN THE YEAR 800 AD
CHARLEMANGE'S CORONATION

𝕴n 800, Charlemagne (768-814), King of France, was knighted Emperor of the Holy Roman Empire by Pope Leo III on Christmas Day. His grandfather, Charles Martel, had stopped the Muslim invasion of Europe at the Battle of Tours in 732 AD.

IN THE YEAR 1000 AD
ST. STEPHEN'S CORONATION

𝕾aint Stephen was crowned apostolic King of Hungary on Christmas Day, in the year 1000. The Pope had sent him a crown and had given him the title of king.

St. Stephen was born a pagan at Pannonia (modern day western Hungary) in the year 969. At the age of 10, he and his father were baptized. At the age of 20, he married Gisela, sister of St. Henry. Stephen later succeeded his father as chief of the Magyars and adopted a policy of Christianization of the country for both political and religious reasons. He suppressed numerous revolts of pagan nobles and welded his tribe into a strong national group.

St. Stephen, apostle of Hungary, died in 1038 and was canonized in 1083. **His pious son, St. Emeric,** was to be the next king, but he died at age 24. St. Emeric **was the namesake of Amerigo Vespucci, the Italian explorer/ mapmaker for whom America was named - Amerigo being the Italianized spelling of Emeric.**

Saint Stephen had written to his son, Emeric:

My dearest son, if you desire to honor the royal crown, I advise, I counsel, I urge you above all things to maintain the Catholic and Apostolic faith with such diligence and care that you may be an example for all those placed under you by God, and that all the clergy may rightly call you a man of true Christian profession. Failing to do this, you may be sure that you will not be called a Christian or a son of the Church.

Indeed, in the royal palace, after the faith itself, the Church holds second place, first constituted and spread through the whole world by His members, the apostles and holy fathers. And though she always produced fresh offspring, nevertheless in certain places she is regarded as ancient.

However, dearest son, even now in our kingdom the Church is proclaimed as young and newly planted; and for that reason she needs more prudent and trustworthy guardians less a benefit which the divine mercy bestowed on us undeservedly should be destroyed and annihilated through your idleness, indolence or neglect.

My beloved son, delight of my heart, hope of your posterity, I pray, I command, that at very time and in everything, strengthened by your devotion to me, you may show favor not only to relations and kin, or to the most eminent, be they leaders or rich men or neighbors or fellow-countrymen, but also to foreigners and to all who come to you.

By fulfilling your duty in this way you will reach the highest state of happiness. Be merciful to all who are suffering violence, keeping always in your heart the example of the Lord who said: "I desire mercy and not sacrifice". Be patient with everyone, not only with the powerful, but also with the weak.

Finally be strong lest prosperity lift you up too much or adversity cast you down. Be humble in this life that God may raise you up in the next. Be truly moderate and do not punish or condemn anyone immoderately. Be gentle so that you may never oppose justice.

Be honorable so that you never voluntarily bring disgrace upon anyone. Be chaste so that you may avoid all the foulness that so resembles the pangs of death. All these virtues I have noted above make up the royal crown and without them no one is fit to rule here on earth or attain to the heavenly Kingdom."

IN THE YEAR 1100 AD "VENI, VENI EMMANUEL"

In the 1100's was written the Latin Christmas hymn, "Veni, Veni Emmanuel":

> Veni, Veni Emmanuel!
> Captivum solve Israel!
> Qui gemit in exsilio,
> Privatus Dei Filio.
> Gaude, gaude, Emmanuel
> Nascetur pro te, Israel.

The song was translated into English in 1851 by John Mason Neale and published in Medieval *Hymns and Sequences*, First Edition. London: Joseph Masters, 1851, pp. 119-120:

> O come, O come, Emmanuel,
> And ransom captive Israel,
> That mourns in lonely exile here
> Until the Son of God appear.
> Rejoice! Rejoice! Emmanuel
> Shall come to thee, O Israel.

IN THE YEAR 1366 AD
"GOOD CHRISTIAN MEN REJOICE"

"Good Christian Men Rejoice" was written by a Dominican, Heinrich Suso (1300-1366), in Ulm, Germany. Folklore has it that Suso, hearing angels sing these words, joined them in a dance of worship. The tune is the 14th century German melody, "In Dulci Jubilo." It was translated from Latin to English by John Mason Neale in *Carols for Christmastide* (London: 1853), and *Christmas Carols Old and New*, 1871.

> Good Christian men, rejoice
> with heart and soul, and voice;
> Give ye heed to what we say:
> News! News!
> Jesus Christ is born today;
> Ox and ass before Him bow;
> and He is in the manger now.

Christ is born today!
Christ is born today!

Good Christian men, rejoice,
with heart and soul and voice;
Now ye hear of endless bliss:
Joy! Joy!
Jesus Christ was born for this!
He has opened the heavenly door,
and man is blest forevermore.
Christ was born for this!
Christ was born for this!

Good Christian men, rejoice,
with heart and soul and voice;
Now ye need not fear the grave:
Peace! Peace!
Jesus Christ was born to save!
Calls you one and calls you all,
to gain His everlasting hall.
Christ was born to save!
Christ was born to save!

Good Christian men, rejoice,
with heart and soul, and voice;
Give ye heed to what we say:
News! News!
Jesus Christ is born today!
Ox and ass before Him bow;
and He is in the manger now.
Christ is born today!
Christ is born today!

Good Christian men, rejoice,
with heart and soul and voice;
Now ye hear of endless bliss:
Joy! Joy!
Jesus Christ was born for this!
He has opened the heavenly door,
and man is blest forevermore.
Christ was born for this!
Christ was born for this!

Good Christian men, rejoice,
with heart and soul and voice;
Now ye need not fear the grave:
Peace! Peace!
Jesus Christ was born to save!
Calls you one and calls you all,
to gain His everlasting hall.
Christ was born to save!
Christ was born to save!

IN THE YEAR 1492 AD
CHRISTOPHER COLUMBUS

On Christmas Eve, December 24, 1492, Christopher Columbus's ship, the Santa Maria, ran aground on the island of Haiti. The ship had to be abandoned and Columbus left 40 men on the island, naming the settlement "La Navidad," meaning "The Nativity." He promised to return the next year. On this same day, Columbus wrote in his Journal to the King and Queen of Spain, stating:

In all the world there can be no better or gentler people. Your Highnesses should feel great joy, because presently they will be Christians, and instructed in the good manners of your realms.

IN THE YEAR 1520 AD
THE CHRISTMAS TREE

The Christmas tree origins trace back to the 200 AD's, when the early church father Tertullian wrote:

You are the light of the world, a tree ever green, if you have renounced the heathen temple.

St. Boniface (680-755), who was also called Wynfred, was the Apostle of the Germans, being sent forth by Pope Gregory II as a missionary to heathen Germany. In the year 716, St. Boniface confronted the Chieftain Gundhar, who was about to offer the little Prince Asulf as a "bloody sacrifice" to Thor, their pagan god who supposedly lived in the huge "donar" oak tree at Geismar.

St. Boniface boldly took an ax and after a few swings at the mighty "blood" oak, an enormous wind blew the tree over. The heathen throng was in awe and converted to Christianity. Then pointing to an evergreen tree that was next to it, or that had miraculously grown up, St. Boniface said:

This is the word, and this is the counsel. Not a drop of blood shall fall tonight, for this is the birth-night of Saint Christ, Son of the All-Father and Saviour of the world. This little tree, a young child of the forest, shall be a home tree tonight.

It is the wood of peace, for your houses are built of fir. It is the sign of endless life, for its branches are ever green. See how it points toward Heaven! Let this be called the tree of the Christ Child; gather about it, not in the wild woods but in your homes; there it will shelter no deeds of blood, but loving gifts and lights of kindness.

Lights at this season can be traced back to the Jewish Festival of Lights, or Feast of the Dedication, in Hebrew called "Hanukkah," where candles were lit to celebrate the driving out of the heathen army of the Syrian king, Antiochus Epiphanes, from Jerusalem in 165 BC by Judas Maccabaeus and the rededication of the Temple.

Antiochus Epiphanes desecrated the temple by using it for idol worship. When the Temple was cleansed of all the pagan defilements, the oil lampstand, known as the menorah, was to be relit. There was a problem, though, as there could only be found enough holy olive oil to burn for one day, and it would take a week before more could be made. The decision was made to pour the small amount in the lamp, and miraculously, it burned for an entire week!

An interesting note is that the New Testament records in John 10:22, that Jesus celebrated it:

And it was at Jerusalem the feast of the dedication, and it was winter. And Jesus walked in the temple in Solomon's porch.

164

In 1520, Martin Luther (1483-1546) was walking on Christmas Eve under the cold December sky and noticed the countless stars illuminating the night. He returned home, and to the delight of his wife and children, set up an evergreen tree placing a great number of small candles on its branches. He used this to tell his children the true meaning of the Christ Child, the Light of the World, whose birth had so gloriously brightened the sky on that first Christmas Eve. He set up a creche scene under the tree so that the lights would appear as the stars above Bethlehem.

IN THE YEAR 1525 AD
"LO, HOW A ROSE E'ER BLOOMING"

Sometime in the early 1500s, the Christmas carol, "Lo, How a Rose E'er Blooming" (Es Ist Ein Ros), was written near Trier, Germany, probably for the Twelfth Night of Christmas.

> Lo, how a rose e'er blooming,
> From tender stem hath sprung!
> From Jesse's lineage coming,
> As men of old have sung.
> It came, a floweret bright,
> Amid the cold of winter
> When half spent was the night
>
> Isaiah 'twas foretold it,
> The Rose I have in mind
> With Mary we behold it,
> The Virgin mother kind

To show God's love aright,
She bore to us a Savior
When half spent was the night

The shepherds heard the story
Proclaimed by angels bright,
How Christ, the Lord of Glory
Was born on earth this night.
To Bethlehem they sped
And in the manger they found him,
As angels heralds said.

This Flower, whose fragrance tender
With sweetness fills the air,
Dispels with glorious splendor
The darkness everywhere;
True man, yet very God,
From Sin and death he saves us,
And lightens every load.

IN THE YEAR 1571
ST. NICHOLAS CATHEDRAL, CYPRUS

St. Nicholas Cathedral in Famagusta was the largest church on the Island of Cyprus. The huge church was begun in 1192, in the French Gothic style of architecture, being dubbed "The Reims of Cyprus." In 1571, 100,000 Muslims, led by Lala Mustafa Pasha, laid siege to Famagusta, which was defended by 6,000 Christians soldiers, led by Venetian Admiral Marco Bragadin.

The courageous defenders held off the Muslim attackers for 10 months, till they surrendered in August of 1571, on the Muslim's promise of amnesty. The Muslim leader, Lala Mustafa Pasha reneged on his promise and cut off the nose and ears of the Venetian Admiral, Marco Bragadin, then flayed him alive and stuffed his skin with straw, parading it around the city. He then killed the 10,000 citizens who had surrendered.

Muslims damaged the St. Nicholas Cathedral during their bombardment, then destroyed all statues, artwork, crucifixes, frescoes, paintings, tombs, and stained glass. They converted the cathedral into the "Mosque of Magusa," and in 1954, renamed it Lala Mustafa Pasha Mosque to honor the brutal Muslim commander.

IN THE YEAR 1600 AD
"I SAW THREE SHIPS"

"**I** Saw Three Ships Come Sailing In" was a popular Christmas carol in England. Sung to the tune "Greensleeves," it was first printed in the 17th century, possibly Derbyshire, England. It was later published in 1833 by William B. Sandys.

The lyrics mention the ships sailing into Bethlehem, but Bethlehem is about 100 from the Sea of Galilee to the northeast or the Mediterranean Sea to the west.

The reference to three ships may have originated with the ships that purportedly brought the relics of the Biblical magi to Cologne Cathedral in the 12th century.

I saw three ships come sailing in
On Christmas Day, on Christmas Day;

I saw three ships come sailing in
On Christmas Day in the morning.

And what was in those ships all three,
On Christmas Day, on Christmas Day?
And what was in those ships all three,
On Christmas Day in the morning?

The Virgin Mary and Christ were there,
On Christmas Day, on Christmas Day;
The Virgin Mary and Christ were there,
On Christmas Day in the morning.

Pray, wither sailed those ships all three,
On Christmas Day, on Christmas Day;
Pray, wither sailed those ships all three,
On Christmas Day in the morning?

O they sailed into Bethlehem,
On Christmas Day, on Christmas Day;
O they sailed into Bethlehem,
On Christmas Day in the morning.

And all the bells on earth shall ring,
On Christmas Day, on Christmas Day;
And all the bells on earth shall ring,
On Christmas Day in the morning.

And all the Angels in Heaven shall sing,
On Christmas Day, on Christmas Day;
And all the Angels in Heaven shall sing,
On Christmas Day in the morning.

And all the souls on earth shall sing,
On Christmas Day, on Christmas Day;
And all the souls on earth shall sing,
On Christmas Day in the morning.

Then let us all rejoice again,
On Christmas Day, on Christmas Day;
Then let us all rejoice again,
On Christmas Day in the morning.

IN THE YEAR 1607 AD
CAPTAIN JOHN SMITH

Captain John Smith recorded that the 40 survivors of the original 100 Virginia settlers gathered in their small chapel Christmas to salute the birth of Christ. The next year their condition improved and they rejoiced in the camp of Indian chieftan Powhatan's son. Captain John Smith wrote:

Never more merrie, nor fedd on more plentie of good oysters, fish, flesh, wild foule and good bread; nor never had better fires in England than in the warm smokie houses.

IN THE YEAR 1624 AD
ST. NICHOLAS & NEW AMSTERDAM

In "Diedrich Knickerbocker's *A History of New York from the Beginning of the New World to the End of the Dutch Dynasty,* 1809, Washington Irving described the excitement in Holland as preparations were made for the first settlers sail to America:

> The delectable accounts given by the great Hendrik Hudson and Master Robert Juet of the country they had discovered excited not a little talk and speculation among the good people of Holland.
>
> Letters patent were granted by Government to an association of merchants, called the West India Company, for the exclusive trade on Hudson River, on which they erected a trading-house called Fort Aurania, or Orange, from whence did spring the great city of Albany...
>
> It was some three or four years after the return of the immortal Hendrik Hudson that a crew of honest Low Dutch colonists set sail from the city of Amsterdam for the shores of America...

Washington Irving wove St. Nicholas, the "Patron Saint of Sailors," into his narrative, as he described the Dutch shipbuilder carving a mascot of St. Nicholas, albeit dressed in a Dutch outfit, into the bow of the ship:

> The ship in which these illustrious adventurers set sail was called the Goede Vrouw, or good woman, in compliment to the wife of the president of the West India Company, who was allowed by everybody, except her husband, to be a sweet-tempered lady—when not in liquor.

It was in truth a most gallant vessel, of the most approved Dutch construction, and made by the ablest ship-carpenters of Amsterdam, who, it is well known, always model their ships after the fair forms of their countrywomen...

The architect, who was somewhat of a religious man, far from decorating the ship with pagan idols, such as Jupiter, Neptune or Hercules, which heathenish abominations, I have no doubt, occasion the misfortunes and shipwreck of many a noble vessel, he I say, on the contrary, did laudably erect for a head, a goodly image of **St. Nicholas**, equipped with a low, broad-brimmed hat, a huge pair of Flemish trunk hose, and a pipe that reached to the end of the bow-sprit.

Thus gallantly furnished, the staunch ship floated sideways, like a majestic goose, out of the harbor of the great city of Amsterdam, and all the bells that were not otherwise engaged, rung a triple bobmajor on the joyful occasion.

Washington Irving recorded the journey:

My great-great-grandfather remarks, that the voyage was uncommonly prosperous, for, being under the especial care of the ever-revered **St. Nicholas**, the Goede Vrouw seemed to be endowed with qualities unknown to common vessels...in consequence of which singular advantage she made out to accomplish her voyage in a very few months, and came to anchor at the mouth of the Hudson, a little to the east of Gibbet Island.

Washington Irving again mentioned St. Nicholas, as colonists looked for a location for their settlement:

Here lifting up their eyes they beheld, on what is at present called the Jersey shore, a small Indian village, pleasantly embowered in a grove of spreading elms, and the natives all collected on the beach, gazing in stupid admiration at the Goede Vrouw.

A boat was immediately dispatched to enter into a treaty with them, and, approaching the shore, hailed them through a trumpet in the most friendly terms; but so horribly confounded were these poor savages at the tremendous and uncouth sound of the Low Dutch language that they one and all took to their heels, and scampered over the Bergen Hills...

Animated by this unlooked-for victory, our valiant heroes sprang ashore in triumph...

On looking about them they were so transported with the excellences of the place that they had very little doubt the blessed **St. Nicholas** had guided them thither as the very spot whereon to settle their colony...which they called by the Indian name Communipaw...

172

Washington Irving begins the strange tale of the "dreamer" Oloffe Van Kortlandt:

> Oloffe Van Kortlandt...Like all land speculators...was much given to dreaming. Never did anything extraordinary happen at Communipaw but he declared that he had previously dreamt it...and was thence aptly denominated Oloffe the Dreamer...
>
> The worthy Van Kortlandt, in the council in question, urged the policy of emerging from the swamps of Communipaw and seeking some more eligible site for the seat of empire.
>
> Such, he said, was the advice of the good **St. Nicholas,** who had appeared to him in a dream the night before, and whom he had known by his broad hat, his long pipe, and the resemblance which he bore to the figure on the bow of the Goede Vrouw.
>
> Many have thought this dream was a mere invention of Oloffe Van Kortlandt, who, it is said, had ever regarded Communipaw with an evil eye, because he had arrived there after all the land had been shared out, and who was anxious to change the seat of empire to some new place, where he might be present at the distribution of "town lots."
>
> But we must not give heed to such insinuations, which are too apt to be advanced against those worthy gentlemen engaged in laying out towns and in other land speculations...

Washington described the Indians and the Dutch settlers:

> The Indians were much given to long talks, and the Dutch to long silence; in this particular, therefore, they accommodated each other completely.
>
> The chiefs would make long speeches about the big bull, the wabash, and the Great Spirit, to which the others would listen very attentively, smoke their pipes, and grunt yah, myn-her; whereat the poor savages were wondrously delighted.
>
> They instructed the new settlers in the best art of curing and smoking tobacco, while the latter in return, made them drunk with true Hollands, and then taught them the art of making bargains...

Washington Irving told as the Dutch were returning from looking for a better place to settle, Oloffe had another "dream" of St. Nicholas:

> Scarce, however, had they gained a distant view of Communipaw, when they were encountered by an obstinate eddy, which opposed their homeward voyage. Weary and dispirited as they were, they yet tugged a feeble oar against the stream; until, as if to settle the strife, half a score of potent billows rolled the tub of Commodore Van Kortlandt high and dry on the long point of an island which divided the bosom of the bay.

Some pretend that these billows were sent by old Neptune to strand the expedition on a spot whereon was to be founded his stronghold in this western world; others, more pious, attribute everything to the guardianship of the good **St. Nicholas**; and after events will be found to corroborate this opinion.

Oloffe Van Kortlandt was a devout trencherman. Every repast was a kind of religious rite with him; and his first thought on finding him once more on dry ground was how he should contrive to celebrate his wonderful escape from Hell-gate and all its horrors by a solemn banquet.

The stores which had been provided for the voyage by the good housewives of Communipaw were nearly exhausted; but in casting his eyes about, the commodore beheld that the shore abounded with oysters. A great store of these was instantly collected; a fire was made at the foot of a tree; all hands fell to roasting, and broiling, and stewing, and frying, and a sumptuous repast was soon set forth. This is thought to be the origin of those civic feasts with which, to the present day, all our public affairs are celebrated, and in which the oyster is ever sure to play an important part...

And the sage Oloffe dreamed a dream—and, lo! the good **St. Nicholas** came riding over the tops of the trees, in that self-same wagon wherein he brings his yearly presents to children. And he descended hard by where the heroes of Communipaw had made their late repast. And he lit his pipe by the fire, and sat himself down and smoked; and as he smoked the smoke from his pipe ascended into the air, and spread like a cloud overhead.

And Oloffe bethought him, and he hastened and climbed up to the top of one of the tallest trees, and saw that the smoke spread over a great extent of country—and as he considered it more attentively he fancied that the great volume of smoke assumed a variety of marvelous forms, where in dim obscurity he saw shadowed out palaces and domes and lofty spires, all of which lasted but a moment, and then faded away, until the whole rolled off, and nothing but the green woods were left.

And when **St. Nicholas** had smoked his pipe he twisted it in his hatband, and laying his finger beside his nose, gave the astonished Van Kortlandt a very significant look, then mounting his wagon, he returned over the treetops and disappeared.

And Van Kortlandt awoke from his sleep greatly instructed, and he aroused his companions, and related to them his dream, and interpreted it that it was the will of **St. Nicholas** that they should settle down and build the city here; and that the smoke of the pipe was a type of how vast would be the extent of the city, inasmuch as the volumes of its smoke would spread over a wide extent of country...

Washington Irving continued:

The great object of their perilous expedition, therefore, being thus happily accomplished, the voyagers returned merrily to Communipaw, where they were received with great rejoicings...

They related the whole history of their voyage, and of the dream of Oloffe Van Kortlandt. And the people lifted up their voices and blessed the good **St. Nicholas**, and from that time forth the sage Van Kortlandt was held in more honor than ever, for his great talent at dreaming, and was pronounced a most useful citizen, and a right good man—when he was asleep...

Washington Irving gives his "tall tale" account of purchasing a spot on Manhattan Island:

As the little squadron from Communipaw drew near to the shores of Manna-hata, a sachem, at the head of a band of warriors, appeared to oppose their landing. Some of the most zealous of the pilgrims were for chastising this insolence with the powder and ball, according to the approved mode of discoverers; but the sage Oloffe gave them the significant sign of **St. Nicholas**, laying his finger beside his nose and winking hard with one eye; whereupon his followers perceived that there was something sagacious in the wind.

He now addressed the Indians in the blandest terms, and made such tempting display of beads, hawks's bells, and red blankets, that he was soon permitted to land, and a great land speculation ensued.

And here let me give the true story of the original purchase of the site of this renowned city, about which so much has been said and written. Some affirm that the first cost was, but sixty guilders.

The learned Dominie Heckwelder records a tradition that the Dutch discoverers bargained for only so much land as the hide of a bullock would cover; but that they cut the hide in strips no thicker than a child's finger, so as to take in a large portion of land, and to take in the Indians into the bargain.

This, however, is an old fable which the worthy Dominie may have borrowed from antiquity. The true version is, that Oloffe Van Kortlandt bargained for just so much land as a man could cover with his nether garments. The terms being concluded, he produced his friend Mynheer Ten Broeck, as the man whose breeches were to be used in measurement.

The simple savages, whose ideas of a man's nether garments had never expanded beyond the dimensions of a breech clout, stared with astonishment and dismay as they beheld this bulbous-bottomed burgher peeled like an onion, and breeches after breeches spread forth over the land until they covered the actual site of this venerable city.

This is the true history of the adroit bargain by which the Island of Manhattan was bought for sixty guilders; and in corroboration of it I will add that Mynheer Ten Breeches, for his services on this memorable occasion, was elevated to the office of land measurer; which he ever afterwards exercised in the colony...

The land being thus fairly purchased of the Indians, a circumstance very unusual in the history of colonization, and strongly illustrative of the honesty of our Dutch progenitors, a stockade fort and trading house were forthwith erected on an eminence in front of the place where the good **St. Nicholas** had appeared in a vision to Oloffe the Dreamer; and which, as has already been observed, was the identical place at present known as the Bowling Green...

Around this fort a progeny of little Dutch-built houses, with tiled roofs and weathercocks, soon sprang up, nestling themselves under its walls for protection, as a brood of half-fledged chickens nestle under the wings of the mother hen. The whole was surrounded by an enclosure of strong palisadoes, to guard against any sudden irruption of the savages.

Outside of these extended the corn-fields and cabbage-gardens of the community, with here and there an attempt at a tobacco plantation; all covering those tracts of country at present called Broadway, Wall Street, William Street, and Pearl Street...

Washington Irving described the Indians:

Thus benignly fostered by the good **St. Nicholas**, the infant city thrived apace. Hordes of painted savages, it is true, still lurked about the unsettled parts of the island. The hunter still pitched his bower of skins and bark beside the rills that ran through the cool and shady glens, while here and there might be seen, on some sunny knoll, a group of Indian wigwams whose smoke arose above the neighboring trees, and floated in the transparent atmosphere.

A mutual good-will, however, existed between these wandering beings and the burghers of New Amsterdam. Our benevolent forefathers endeavored as much as possible to ameliorate their situation, by giving them gin, rum, and glass beads, in exchange for their peltries; for it seems the kind-hearted Dutchmen had conceived a great friendship for their savage neighbors, on account of their being pleasant men to trade with, and little skilled in the art of making a bargain.

Now and then a crew of these half human sons of the forest would make their appearance in the streets of New Amsterdam, fantastically painted and decorated with beads and flaunting feathers, sauntering about with an air of listless indifference—sometimes in the marketplace, instructing the little Dutch boys in the use of the bow and arrow—at other times, inflamed with liquor, swaggering, and whooping, and yelling about the town like so many fiends, to the great dismay of all the good wives, who would hurry their children into the house, fasten the doors, and throw water upon the enemy from the garret windows...

In 1647, Peter Stuyvesant (1612-1672), having one wooden leg, became the Governor of the Dutch West India Company Colony, as Washington Irving described:

> Such was Peter Stuyvesant, and if my admiration of him has on this occasion transported my style beyond the sober gravity which becomes the philosophic recorder of historic events, I must plead as an apology that though a little grey-headed Dutchman, arrived almost at the down-hill of life, I still retain a lingering spark of that fire which kindles in the eye of youth when contemplating the virtues of ancient worthies. Blessed thrice, and nine times blessed be the good **St. Nicholas**, if I have indeed escaped that apathy which chills the sympathies of age and paralyses every glow of enthusiasm...

Washington Irving talked about rumors of witches, superstitious Dutch settlers, and St. Nicholas:

> When treating of these tempestuous times, the unknown writer of the Stuyvesant manuscript breaks out into an apostrophe in praise of the good **St. Nicholas**, to whose protecting care he ascribes the dissensions which broke out in the council of the league, and the direful witchcraft which filled all Yankee land as with Egyptian darkness.
>
> A portentous gloom, says he, hung lowering over the fair valleys of the east; the pleasant banks of the Connecticut no longer echoed to the sounds of rustic gayety; grisly phantoms glided about each wild brook and silent glen; fearful apparitions were seen in the air; strange voices were heard in solitary places, and the border towns were so occupied in detecting and punishing losel witches, that for a time all talk of war was suspended, and New Amsterdam and its inhabitants seemed to be totally forgotten.
>
> I must not conceal the fact, that at one time there was some danger of this plague of witchcraft extending into the New Netherlands; and certain witches, mounted on broomsticks, are said to have been seen whisking in the air over some of the Dutch villages near the borders; but the worthy Nederlanders took the precaution to nail horse-shoes to their doors, which it is well

known are effectual barriers against all diabolical vermin of the kind.

Many of those horse-shoes may be seen at this very day on ancient mansions and barns, remaining from the days of the patriarchs; nay, the custom is still kept up among some of our legitimate Dutch yeomanry, who inherit from their forefathers a desire to keep witches and Yankees out of the country.

Washington Irving told of Peter Stuyvesant and the Dutch settlers controversies with Swedish settlers in 1655:

The attentive reader will recollect that certain freebooting Swedes had become very troublesome in this quarter in the latter part of the reign of William the Testy, setting at naught the proclamations of that veritable potentate, and putting his admiral, the intrepid Jan Jensen Alpendam, to a perfect nonplus.

To check the incursions of these Swedes, Peter Stuyvesant now ordered a force to that frontier, giving the command of it to General Jacobus Van Poffenburgh, an officer who had risen to great importance during the reign of Wilhelmus Kieft...

Such was the famous mosquito war on the Delaware, of which General Van Poffenburgh would fain have been the hero; but the devout people of the Nieuw-Nederlands always ascribed the discomfiture of the Swedes to the miraculous intervention of **St. Nicholas**...

Washington Irving described Governor Peter Stuyvesant leaving to confront the Swedes:

> Upon beholding this, the great Peter...determined to wait no longer for the tardy assistance of these oily citizens, but to muster up his merry men of the Hudson, who, brought up among woods, and wilds, and savage beasts, like our yeomen of Kentucky, delighted in nothing so much as desperate adventures and perilous expeditions through the wilderness.
>
> Thus resolving, he ordered his trusty squire, Antony Van Corlear, to have his state galley prepared and duly victualed; which being performed, he attended public service at the great church of **St. Nicholas**, like a true and pious governor; and then leaving peremptory orders with his council to have the chivalry of the Manhattoes marshaled out and appointed against his return, departed upon his recruiting voyage up the waters of the Hudson...
>
> Let us, then, commit the dauntless Peter, his brave galley, and his loyal crew, to the protection of the blessed **St. Nicholas**, who, I have no doubt, will prosper him in his voyage, while we await his return at the great city of New Amsterdam...

Washington Irving described a pseudo battle with the Swedes to take back their Dutch fort:

A heavy gloom hung over the late bustling city; the honest burghers smoked their pipes in profound thoughtfulness, casting many a wistful look to the weathercock on the church of **St. Nicholas**; and all the old women, having no longer the presence of Peter Stuyvesant to hearten them, gathered their children home, and barricaded the doors and windows every evening at sun down...

The choleric Peter, indignant at having his rightful fort so treacherously taken from him (by Swedish settlers), and thus pertinaciously withheld, refused the proposed armistice, and swore by the pipe of **St. Nicholas**, which, like the sacred fire, was never extinguished, that unless the fort were surrendered in ten minutes, he would incontinently storm the works, make all the garrison run the gauntlet, and split their scoundrel of a commander like a pickled shad.

To give this menace the greater effect, he drew forth his trusty sword, and shook it at them with such a fierce and vigorous motion that doubtless, if it had not been exceeding rusty, it would have lightened terror into the eyes and hearts of the enemy.

He then ordered his men to bring a broadside to bear upon the fort, consisting of two swivels, three muskets, a long duck fowling-piece, and two braces of horse-pistols.

Therefore stand by for broken heads and bloody noses! My pen hath long itched for a battle—siege after siege have I carried on without blows or bloodshed; but now I have at length got a chance, and I vow to Heaven and **St. Nicholas** that, let the chronicles of the times say what they please, neither Sallust, Livy, Tacitus, Polybius, nor any other historian did ever record a fiercer fight than that in which my valiant chieftains are now about to engage.

For an instant the mighty Peter paused in the midst of his career, and mounting on a stump, addressed his troops in eloquent Low Dutch, exhorting them to fight like duyvels, and assuring them that if they conquered, they should get plenty of booty; if they fell, they should be allowed the satisfaction, while dying, of reflecting that it was in the service of their country; and after they were dead, of seeing their names inscribed in the temple of renown, and handed down, in company with all the other great men of the year, for the admiration of posterity...

Then lugging out his trusty sabre, he brandished it three times over his head, ordered Van Corlear to sound a charge, and shouting the words, "**St. Nicholas** and the Manhattoes!" courageously dashed forwards.

His warlike followers, who had employed the interval in lighting their pipes, instantly stuck them into their mouths, gave a furious puff, and charged gallantly under cover of the smoke.

The Swedes followed up their fire by leaping the counterscarp, and falling tooth and nail upon the foe with furious outcries. And now might be seen prodigies of valor, unmatched in history or song.

Here was the sturdy Stoffel Brinkerhoff brandishing his quarter-staff like the giant Blanderon his oak tree (for he scorned to carry any other weapon), and drumming a horrific tune upon the hard heads of the Swedish soldiery. There were the Van Kortlandts, posted at a distance, like the Locrian archers of yore, and plying it most potently with the long-bow, for which they were so justly renowned.

On a rising knoll were gathered the valiant men of Sing-Sing, assisting marvellously in the fight, by chanting the great song of **St. Nicholas**; but as to the Gardeniers of Hudson, they were absent on a marauding party, laying waste the neighboring water-melon patches...

But what, O Muse! was the rage of Peter Stuyvesant, when from afar he saw his army giving way! In the transports of his wrath he sent forth a roar, enough to shake the very hills. The men of the Manhattoes plucked up new courage at the sound; or rather, they rallied at the voice of their leader, of whom they stood more in awe than of all the Swedes in Christendom.

Without waiting for their aid, the daring Peter dashed, sword in hand, into the thickest of the foe. Then might be seen achievements worthy of the days of the giants. Wherever he went, the enemy shrank before him; the Swedes fled to right and left, or were driven, like dogs, into their own ditch; but, as he pushed forward singly with headlong courage, the foe closed behind and hung upon his rear.

One aimed a blow full at his heart; but the protecting power which watches over the great and the good turned aside the hostile blade, and directed it to a side pocket, where reposed an enormous iron tobacco-box, endowed, like the shield of Achilles, with supernatural powers, doubtless from bearing the portrait of the blessed **St. Nicholas**.

Peter Stuyvesant turned like an angry bear upon the foe, and seizing him as he fled, by an immeasurable queue, "Ah, whoreson caterpillar," roared he, "here's what shall make worms' meat of thee!" So saying, he whirled his sword, and dealt a blow that would have decapitated the varlet, but that the pitying steel struck short, and shaved the queue for ever from his crown...

The good Peter reeled with the blow, and turning up his eyes, beheld a thousand suns, beside moons and stars, dancing about the firmament; at length, missing his footing, by reason of his wooden leg, down he came on his seat of honor with a crash which shook the surrounding hills, and might have wrecked his frame had he not been received into a cushion softer than velvet, which Providence or Minerva, or **St. Nicholas**, or some kindly cow, had benevolently prepared for his reception.

Thanks to **St. Nicholas**, we have safely finished this tremendous battle. Let us sit down, my worthy reader, and cool ourselves, for I am in a prodigious sweat and agitation. Truly this fighting of battles is hot work!...

But since the various records I consulted did not warrant it, I had too much conscience to kill a single soldier. By **St. Nicholas**, but it would have been a pretty piece of business!...And now, gentle reader, that we are tranquilly sitting down here, smoking our pipes, permit me to indulge in a melancholy reflection which at this moment passes across my mind...

Washington Irving told how Governor Peter Stuyvesant promoted holidays, like that of **St. Nicholas**:

From what I have recounted in the foregoing chapter, I would not have it imagined that the great Peter was a tyrannical potentate, ruling with a rod of iron.

On the contrary, where the dignity of office permitted, he abounded in generosity and condescension.

If he refused the brawling multitude the right of misrule, he at least endeavored to rule them in righteousness.

To spread abundance in the land, he obliged the bakers to give thirteen loaves to the dozen—a golden rule which remains a monument of his beneficence...

He delighted to see the poor and the laboring man rejoice; and for this purpose he was a great promoter of holidays.

Under his reign there was a great cracking of eggs at Paas or Easter; Whitsuntide or Pinxter (Pentecost) also flourished in all its bloom; and never were stockings better filled on the eve of the blessed **St. Nicholas**.

But come what may, I here pledge my veracity that in all warlike conflicts and doubtful perplexities he will every acquit himself like a gallant, noble-minded, obstinate old cavalier.

Forward, then, to the charge! Shine out, propitious stars, on the renowned city of the Manhattoes; and the blessing of **St. Nicholas** go with thee, honest Peter Stuyvesant.

In 1664, the British King Charles II sent his brother James, the Duke of York, to claim the Dutch city of New Amsterdam for the English.

Gallant, but unfortunate Peter! Did I not enter with sad forebodings on this ill-starred expedition?

Did I not tremble when I saw thee, with no other councillor than thine own head; no other armour but an honest tongue, a spotless conscience, and a rusty sword; no other protector but **St. Nicholas**, and no other attendant but a trumpeter—did I not tremble when I beheld thee thus sally forth to contend with all the knowing powers of New England?

Thus did this venerable assembly of sages lavish away their time, which the urgency of affairs rendered invaluable, in empty brawls and long-winded speeches, without ever agreeing, except on the point with which they started, namely, that there was no time to be lost, and delay was ruinous.

At length, **St. Nicholas** taking compassion on their distracted situation, and anxious to preserve them from anarchy, so ordered, that in the midst of one of their most noisy debates on the subject of fortification and defence, when they had nearly fallen to loggerheads in consequence of not being able to convince each other, the question was happily settled by the sudden entrance of a messenger, who informed them that a hostile fleet had arrived, and was actually advancing up the bay!

On September 8, 1664, the English took control of New Amsterdam. The Dutch settlers chose to surrender rather than fight. Some complained that Governor Peter Stuyvesant was too strict and would rather let the British rule, as Washington Irving related:

> The sovereign people crowded into the marketplace, herding together with the instinct of sheep, who seek safety in each other's company when the shepherd and his dog are absent, and the wolf is prowling round the fold. Far from finding relief, however, they only increased each other's terrors.
>
> Each man looked ruefully in his neighbor's face, in search of encouragement, but only found in its woebegone lineaments a confirmation of his own dismay. Not a word now was to be heard of conquering Great Britain, not a whisper about the sovereign virtues of economy—while the old women heightened the general gloom by clamorously bewailing their fate, and calling for protection on **St. Nicholas** and Peter Stuyvesant...
>
> As soon as the burgomasters could recover from their confusion, and had time to breathe, they called a public meeting, where they related at full length, and with appropriate coloring and exaggeration, the despotic and vindictive deportment of the

governor, declaring that, for their own parts, they did not value a straw the being kicked, cuffed, and mauled by the timber toe of his excellency, but that they felt for the dignity of the sovereign people, thus rudely insulted by the outrage committed on the seat of honor of their representatives.

The latter part of the harangue came home at once to that delicacy of feeling and jealous pride of character vested in all true mobs; who, though they may bear injuries without a murmur, yet are marvelously jealous of their sovereign dignity; and there is no knowing to what act of resentment they might have been provoked, had they not been somewhat more afright of their sturdy old governor than they were of **St. Nicholas**, the English, or the d——l himself...

Washington Irving described the terms of the surrender of New Amsterdam:

While all these struggles and dissentions were prevailing in the unhappy city of New Amsterdam, and while its worthy but ill-starred governor was framing the above quoted letter, the English commanders did not remain idle.

They had agents secretly employed to foment the fears and clamors of the populace; and moreover circulated far and wide through the adjacent country a proclamation, repeating the terms they had already held out in their summons to surrender, at the same time beguiling the simple Nederlanders with the most crafty and conciliating professions.

They promised that every man who voluntarily submitted to the authority of his British Majesty should retain peaceful possession of his house, his vrouw (wife), and his cabbage-garden.

That he should be suffered to smoke his pipe, speak Dutch, wear as many beeches as he pleased, and import bricks, tiles, and stone jugs from Holland, instead of manufacturing them on the spot.

That he should on no account be compelled to learn the English language, nor eat codfish on Saturdays, nor keep accounts in any other way than by casting them up on his fingers, and chalking them down upon the crown of his hat; as is observed among the Dutch yeomanry at the present day.

That every man should be allowed quietly to inherit his father's hat, coat, shoe-buckles, pipe, and every other personal appendage; and that no man should be obliged to conform to any improvements, inventions, or any other modern innovations; but, on the contrary, should be permitted to build his house, follow his trade, manage his farm, rear his hogs, and educate his children, precisely as his ancestors had done before him from time immemorial.

Finally, that he should have all the benefits of free trade, and should not be required to acknowledge any other saint in the calendar than **St. Nicholas**, who should thenceforward, as before, be considered the tutelar saint of the city...

Washington Irving told how Governor Peter Stuyvesant firmly resisted signing the surrender agreement, until, upon the insistence of Dutch citizens, he relented on September 8, 1664:

Commissioners were now appointed on both sides, and a capitulation was speedily arranged; all that was wanting to ratify it was that it should be signed by the governor.

When the commissioners waited upon him for this purpose they were received with grim and bitter courtesy.

His warlike accoutrements were laid aside; an old Indian night-gown was wrapped about his rugged limbs; a red nightcap overshadowed his frowning brow; an iron-grey beard of three days' growth gave additional grimness to his visage.

Thrice did he seize a worn-out stump of a pen, and essay to sign the loathsome paper; thrice did he clinch his teeth, and make a horrible countenance, as though a dose of rhubarb-senna, and ipecacuanha, had been offered to his lips.

At length, dashing it from him, he seized his brass-hilted sword, and jerking it from the scabbard, swore by **St. Nicholas** to sooner die than yield to any power under heaven.

For two whole days did he persist in this magnanimous resolution, during which his house was besieged by the rabble, and menaces and clamorous revilings exhausted to no purpose. And now another course was adopted to soothe, if possible, his mighty ire.

A procession was formed by the burgomasters and schepens, followed by the populace, to bear the capitulation in state to the governor's dwelling. They found the castle strongly barricaded, and the old hero in full regimentals, with his cocked hat on his head, posted with a blunderbuss at the garret window...

After the surrender, New Amsterdam became New York, named after James, the Duke of York. Governor Peter Stuyvesant sailed to Holland to explain what happened, then later returned to the colony he had helped build. Washington Irving wrote how in his mansion, the former Governor continued to celebrate the day of **St. Nicholas**:

The good old Dutch festivals, those periodical demonstrations of an overflowing heart and a thankful spirit, which are falling into sad disuse among my fellow citizens, were faithfully observed in the mansion of Governor Stuyvesant.

New year was truly a day of open-handed liberality, of jocund revelry and warm-hearted congratulation, when the bosom swelled with genial good-fellowship, and the plenteous table was attended with an unceremonious freedom and honest broad-mouthed merriment unknown in these days of degeneracy and refinement.

Paas (Easter) and Pinxter (Pentecost) were scrupulously observed throughout his dominions; nor was the day of **St. Nicholas** suffered to pass by without making presents, hanging the stocking in the chimney, and complying with all its other ceremonies...

Washington Irving reminisced of Governor Peter Stuyvesant after his death:

With sad and gloomy countenances the multitude gathered round the grave of Peter Stuyvesant. They dwelt with mournful hearts on the sturdy virtues, the signal services, and the gallant exploits of the brave old worthy.

They recalled, with secret upbraiding, their own factious oppositions to his government; and many an ancient burgher, whose phlegmatic features had never been known to relax, nor his eyes to moisten, was now observed to puff a pensive pipe, and the big drop to steal down his cheek; while he muttered, with affectionate accent, and melancholy shake of the head, "Well, den!—Hardkoppig Peter ben gone at last!"...

His remains were deposited in the family vault, under a chapel which he had piously erected on his estate, and dedicated to **St. Nicholas**, and which stood on the identical spot at present occupied by St. Mark's church, where his tombstone is still to be seen.

His estate, or bowery, as it was called, has ever continued in the possession of his descendants, who, by the uniform integrity of their conduct, and their strict adherence to the customs and manners that prevailed in the "good old times," have proved themselves worthy of their illustrious ancestor.

In an interesting twist, just as the Duke of York, and disgruntled Dutch settlers, forced the Dutch Governor Peter Stuyvesant to give up his rule of New Amsterdam in 1664, so the Duke of York, who later became King James II of England, was forced to give up his rule of the British Empire by the Dutch Prince William of Orange and disgruntled British subjects in 1689. This was called The Glorious Revolution of William and Mary.

IN THE YEAR 1625 AD
JOHN DONNE

On Christmas day, 1625, John Donne declared:

Now God comes to thee, not as in the dawning of the day, not as in the bud of the spring, but as the sun at noon to illustrate all shadows, as the sheaves in harvest, to fill all penuries, all occasions invite his mercies, and all times are his seasons.

IN THE YEAR 1625 AD
TWELVE DAYS OF CHRISTMAS

The popular song "The Twelve Days of Christmas" was possibly inspired by the 1625 song titled "In Those Twelve Days," where a meaning was assigned to each day:

What are they that are but one?
We have one God alone...
What are they which are by two?
Two testaments, Old and New...
What are they which are but three?
Three persons in the Trinity...
What are they which are but four?
Four sweet Evangelists there are...
What are they which are but five?
Five senses...
What are they which are but six?
Six days to labor...
What are they which are but seven?
Seven liberal arts hath God sent down...
What are they which are but eight?
Eight Beatitudes...
What are they which are but nine?

Nine Muses...with sacred tunes...
What are they which are but ten?
Ten statutes God to Moses gave...
What are they which are but eleven?
Eleven thousand virgins...
suffered death for Jesus' sake.
What are they which are but twelve?
Twelve attending on God's son.

This is a possible origin of the song, "The Twelve Days of Christmas." In England, during the 1600's, there was much religious persecution. It was dangerous to openly teach doctrines of faith, as the religious climate fluctuated frequently. As a result, spiritual lessons for children were put into songs with symbolic meanings, similar to Sunday School songs. A tradition is that the song "The Twelve Days of Christmas" was composed during this period:

On the twelfth day of Christmas,
my true love gave to me...
12 Drummers Drumming
11 Pipers Piping
10 Lords-a-Leaping
9 Ladies Dancing
8 Maids-a-Milking
7 Swans-a-Swimming
6 Geese-a-Laying
5 Gold Rings
4 Calling Birds
3 French Hens
2 Turtle Doves
And a Partridge in a Pear Tree.

An explanation of the song's possible meaning is:

My True Love	God Himself
A Partridge	Jesus Christ
(A partridge will	("He was wounded
feign injury to	for our transgressions;
decoy predators	He was bruised
from helpless	for our iniquities."
nestlings)	Isaiah 53:5)
Pear Tree	Cross & Tree of Adam's fall
2 Turtle Doves	Old & New Testaments
3 French Hens	Faith, Hope & Love
4 Calling Birds	Four Gospels
5 Golden Rings	Pentateuch-First 5 Books of Bible
6 Geese A-Laying	Six Days of Creation
7 Swans a-Swimming	Seven Gifts of the Holy Spirit
8 Maids A-Milking	Eight Beatitudes
9 Ladies Dancing	Nine Fruits of the Holy Spirit
10 Lords A-Leaping	Ten Commandments
11 Pipers Piping	Eleven Faithful Apostles
12 Drummers	Twelve Points in Apostles Creed

IN THE YEAR 1678 AD
FATHER JACQUES MARQUETTE

𝔉ather Jacques Marquette (1637-1675) had been the French missionary-explorer of Lake Michigan, the Mississippi River, and the Illinois region. In an account, *The Death of Marquette*, published 1678 by Father Claude Dablon, Superior of Missions, Society of Jesus, Canada, was written:

Sometime after Christmas, in order to obtain the grace not to die without having taken possession of his beloved mission, he invited his companions to make a novena in honor of the Immaculate Conception of the Blessed Virgin.

Contrary to all human expectation, he was heard, and, recovering, found himself able to proceed to the Illinois town as soon as navigation was free. This he accomplished in great joy, setting out on the 29th of March.

He was eleven days on the way, where he had ample matter for suffering, both from his still sickly state and from the severity and inclemency of the weather.

Having at last reached the town on the 8th of April, he was received there as an angel from heaven; and after having several times assembled the chiefs of the nation with all the old men (anciens), to sow in their minds the first seed of the gospel, after carrying his instructions into the cabins, which were always filled with crowds of people, he resolved to speak to all publicly in general assembly, he convoked in the open fields, the cabins being too small for the meeting.

A beautiful prairie near the town was chosen for the great council. It was adorned in the fashion of the country, being spread with mats and bear-skins; and the father, having hung on cords some pieces of India taffety, attached to them four large pictures of the

Blessed Virgin, which were thus visible on all sides.

The auditory was composed of five hundred chiefs and old men, seated in a circle around the father, while the youth stood without to the number of fifteen hundred, not counting women and children who are very numerous, the town being composed of five or six hundred fires.

The father spoke to all this gathering, and addressed them ten words by ten presents which he made them; he explained to them the principal mysteries of our religion, and the end for which he had come to their country; and especially he preached to them Christ crucified, for it was the very eve of the great day on which he died on the cross for them, as well as for the rest of men. He then said mass.

IN THE YEAR 1700 AD
NAHUM TATE

Nahum Tate (1652-1715), was honored by England's royalty with the title of poet-laureate, December 24, 1692. He was acclaimed for his version of Shakespeare's *King Lear*, and for co-authoring Dryden's *Absalom and Achitopel*. In 1700, Nahum Tate wrote in "Christmas Hymn":

Shepherds watched their flocks by night,
All seated on the ground,

The angel of the Lord came down,
And glory shone around.

IN THE YEAR 1719 AD
"JOY TO THE WORLD"

𝕴n the year 1707, Isaac Watts (1674-1748) wrote a
Christmas carol based on Psalm 98, titled, "Joy to the
World." It was first published in 1719 in Watts' collection,
*The Psalms of David: Imitated in the language of the New
Testament, and applied to the Christian state and worship.*
As of the late 20th century, "Joy to the World" was the most-
published Christmas hymn in North America:

> Joy to the world! The Lord is come;
> Let earth receive her King;
> Let every heart prepare him room,
> And heaven and nature sing,
> And heaven and nature sing,
> And heaven, and heaven, and nature sing.

> Joy to the world! The Saviour reigns;
> Let men their songs employ;
> While fields and floods, rocks, hills, and plains
> Repeat the sounding joy,
> Repeat the sounding joy,
> Repeat, repeat the sounding joy.

> No more let sins and sorrows grow,
> Nor thorns infest the ground;
> He comes to make His blessings flow

Far as the curse is found,
Far as the curse is found,
Far as, far as, the curse is found.

He rules the world with truth and grace,
And makes the nations prove
The glories of His righteousness,
And wonders of His love,
And wonders of His love,
And wonders, wonders, of His love.

IN THE YEAR 1739 AD
"HARK! THE HERALD ANGELS SING"

Charles Wesley wrote "Hark! The Herald Angels Sing." He was the 18th child of Rev. Samuel and Susanna Wesley, born December 18, 1707, at Epworth, England. He excelled in school and came to the attention of Garret Wesley, or Wellesley, a Member of Parliament with a large fortune in Daugan, Ireland. Having no child, he offered to adopt Charles as his heir, but Charles declined.

After graduating from Oxford, Charles sailed to the colony of Georgia as secretary to the colony's founder, General James Oglethorpe.

In 1717, Oglethorpe had fought the Muslim Turks who were attacking Belgrade, Serbia. Afterwards, he returned to England and entered Parliament. In 1732, James Oglethorpe founded the Colony of Georgia in America, with Charles Wesley serving as his secretary.

Charles Wesley's brother, John Wesley, served as the Anglican minister for the Colony. The Wesleys' desire to minister to Indians never materialized so they returned to England where their preaching started the Great Awakening Revival. John founded the Methodist Church and Charles wrote over 6,000 hymns.

In 1739, Charles Wesley wrote "Hark! The Herald Angels Sing." The carol was put the music of Lutheran composer Felix Mendelssohn, grandson of the notable Jewish philosopher, Moses Mendelssohn:

> Hark! The herald angels sing
> "Glory to the newborn King!
> Peace on earth, and mercy mild;
> God and sinners reconciled."
> Joyful, all ye nations, rise,
> Join the triumph of the skies;
> With the angelic host proclaim:
> "Christ is born in Bethlehem,"
> Hark! The herald angels sing,
> "Glory to the newborn King!"
>
> Christ by highest heav'n adored,
> Christ the everlasting Lord!
> Late in time, behold Him come,
> Offspring of a Virgin's womb,
> Veiled in flesh the Godhead see,
> Hail the incarnate Deity!
> Pleased as man with man to dwell,
> Jesus, our Emmanuel,
> Hark! The herald angels sing,
> "Glory to the newborn King!"

Hail the heav'n-born Prince of Peace!
Hail the Son of Righteousness!
Light and life to all He brings,
Ris'n with healing in His wings.
Mild He lays His glory by,
Born that man no more may die,
Born to raise the sons of earth,
Born to give them second birth.
Hark! The herald angels sing,
"Glory to the newborn King!"

IN THE YEAR 1740 AD
"O COME, ALL YE FAITHFUL"

"O Come, All Ye Faithful" was originally written
in Latin as *Adeste Fideles*. It is attributed to John F. Wade,
with the music by John Reading in the early 1700s, and first
published in a collection known as *Cantus Diversi* in 1751.

O come, all ye faithful,
Joyful and triumphant,
O come ye, O come ye,
to Bethlehem.
Come and behold Him,
Born the King of angels! (Chorus)

O come, let us adore Him,
O come, let us adore Him,
O come, let us adore Him,
Christ the Lord.

God of God,
Light of Light,
Lo! he abhors not the Virgin's womb;
Very God, Begotten not created. (Chorus)

Sing, choirs of angels,
Sing in exultation;
Sing, all ye citizens of heaven above!
Glory to God, In the highest; (Chorus)

Yea, Lord, we greet Thee,
Born this happy morning;
Jesu, to Thee be glory given;
Word of the Father,
Now in flesh appearing. (Chorus)

IN THE YEAR 1741 AD
HANDEL'S MESSIAH

In the mid 1700's, George Frideric Handel was at the low point of his career and was suffering partial paralysis on his left side due to a stroke. Incredibly, beginning August 22, 1741, Handel composed the Messiah in only 21 days, as part of a series of concerts in Dublin to benefit charities. The premiere was met with overwhelming success. When it was performed in London, King George II stood to his feet during the singing of the "Hallelujah" Chorus.

IN THE YEAR 1745 AD
BENJAMIN FRANKLIN

There Really is a Santa Claus

𝔅enjamin Franklin's axioms are contained in his *Maxims and Morals*, such as:

> Let no pleasure tempt thee,
> no profit allure thee,
> no ambition corrupt thee,
> no example sway thee,
> no persuasion move thee to do anything
> which thou knowest to be evil;
> so thou shalt live jollily,
> for a good conscience
> is a continual Christmas.

IN THE YEAR 1745 AD
YOUNG GEORGE WASHINGTON

𝔍n 1745, at thirteen years of age, George Washington copied some verses on "Christmas Day":

> Assist me, Muse divine, to sing the Morn,
> On Which the Saviour of Mankind was born.

IN THE YEAR 1760 AD
"GOD REST YE MERRY, GENTLEMEN"

"𝔊od Rest Ye Merry, Gentlemen" was first published on a broadsheet in London circa 1760 as a "New Christmas carol." ("Three New Christmas Carols," printed and sold at the printing-office on Bow Church-Yard, London).

It was later published as an arrangement for Piano Forte by Samuel Wesley in London sometime before 1815, and in 1833 by William B. Sandys. It was called "the most common and generally popular of all carol tunes," and even referred to in Charles Dickens' *A Christmas Carol*, 1843:

> ...at the first sound of — 'God bless you, merry gentlemen! May nothing you dismay!'— Scrooge seized the ruler with such energy of action, that the singer fled in terror, leaving the keyhole to the fog and even more congenial frost.

> God rest ye merry, gentlemen,
> Let nothing you dismay.
> For Jesus Christ our Savior,
> Was born on Christmas Day;
> To save us all from Satan's power,
> When we were gone astray. (Chorus)

> O tidings of comfort and joy,
> For Jesus Christ our Savior
> Was born on Christmas day.

> In Bethlehem, in Jury,
> This blessed Babe was born,
> And laid within a manger,
> Upon this blessed morn;
> The which His mother Mary
> Did nothing take in scorn. (Chorus)

> From God our heavenly Father,
> A blessed angel came.

And unto certain shepherds,
Brought tidings of the same,
How that in Bethlehem was born,
The Son of God by name: (Chorus)

Fear not, then said the Angel,
Let nothing you affright,
This day is born a Savior,
Of virtue, power, and might;
So frequently to vanquish all,
The friends of Satan quite; (Chorus)

The shepherds at those tidings,
Rejoiced much in mind,
And left their flocks a feeding,
In tempest, storm, and wind,
And went to Bethlehem straightway,
This blessed babe to find: (Chorus)

But when to Bethlehem they came,
Whereas this infant lay
They found him in a manger,
Where oxen feed on hay;
His mother Mary kneeling,
Unto the Lord did pray: (Chorus)

With sudden joy and gladness
The shepherds were beguiled,
To see the Babe if Israel,
Before His mother mild,
O then with joy and cheerfulness
Rejoice, each mother's child. (Chorus)

Now to the Lord sing praises,
All you within this place,
And with true love and brotherhood,
Each other now embrace;
This holy tide of Christmas,
Doth bring redeeming grace. (Chorus)

God bless the ruler of this house,
And send him long to reign,
And many a merry Christmas
May live to see again;
Among your friends and kindred
That live both far and near.

IN THE YEAR 1766 AD
VIRGINIA ALMANACK

In 1766, the *Virginia Almanack* wrote:

Now Christmas comes, 'tis fit that we
Should feast and sing, and merry be:
Keep open the house, let fidlers play.
A fig for cold, sing care away;

IN THE YEAR 1774 AD
WASHINGTON PREPARED FOR WAR

The book, *The Real George Washington-The Man Who United America*, by Jay A. Parry and Andrew M. Allison, records:

There Really is a Santa Claus

Washington returned home at the end of October 1774. The plight of the colonies continued to weigh heavily on his mind. After a quiet Christmas season, he met in mid-January with George Mason and others to establish a military association in Fairfax County.

Many other colonial militias were established at the same time, as local leaders responded to the resolves of Congress. During the next two months, Washington several times made the eight-mile trip to Alexandria to drill the green Fairfax militia.

IN THE YEAR 1776 AD
BATTLE OF TRENTON

The first six months of the Revolution saw the Continental Army chased out of New York, across New Jersey, and into Pennsylvania. Ranks dwindled from 20,000 to 2,000 exhausted soldiers- most leaving at year's end when their six-month enlistment was up.

Expecting a British invasion, the Continental Congress fled Philadelphia and sent the word: "Until Congress shall otherwise order, General Washington shall be possessed of full power to order and direct all things."

In a desperate military operation, with the password "Victory or Death," Washington's troops crossed the ice-filled Delaware River at midnight Christmas Day. Trudging in a blinding blizzard, with one soldier freezing to death, they attacked the feared Hessian troops at Trenton, New

Jersey, on daybreak December 26, 1776, capturing nearly a thousand in just over an hour. A few Americans were shot and wounded, including James Monroe, the future 5th President.

Woodrow Wilson, in his *History of the American People*, wrote:

> What there was to be done he did himself. The British stopped at the Delaware; but their lines reached Burlington, within eighteen miles of Philadelphia, and from Trenton, which they held in some force, extended through Princeton to New Brunswick and their headquarters at New York. Philadelphia was stricken with utter panic.

> Sick and ragged soldiers poured in from Washington's camp, living evidences of what straits he was in, and had to be succored and taken care of; the country roads were crowded with vehicles leaving the town laden with women and children and household goods; the Congress itself incontinently fled the place and betook itself to Baltimore.

> Washington's military stores were in the town, but he could get no proper protection for them. It was at that very moment, nevertheless, that he showed all the world with what skill and audacity he could strike. By dint of every resolute and persistent effort he had before Christmas brought his little force to a fighting strength of some six thousand.

More than half of these were men enlisted only until the new year should open, but he moved before that. During the night of Christmas Day, 1776, ferried by doughty fishermen from far Gloucester and Marblehead,-the same hardy fellows who had handled his boats the night he abandoned the heights of Brooklyn,-he got twenty-five hundred men across the river through pitchy darkness and pounding ice; and in the early light and frost of the next morning he took Trenton, with its garrison of nine hundred Hessians, at the point of the bayonet.

The book, *The Real George Washington-The Man Who United America*, by Jay A. Parry and Andrew M. Allison, describes General George Washington's perilous crossing:

The Americans celebrated apprehensively on Christmas Day, but the Hessians were carefree and self-secure. Colonel Johann Rall, commander of the Hessians at Trenton and a hero from the capture of Fort Washington, spent Christmas evening in a supper party, then called for wine and cards.

The night storm howled around the home of the wealthy local merchant with whom he was visiting, but Rall paid it no heed. Was not this the night of the Nativity, the time for gaiety and celebration? He put the cares of war far from him. He had sentries posted along the roads, and they would certainly notify him if the Americans made a move. Besides, what army would be foolish enough to venture out on a stormy night like this?

As the cold evening darkened, Washington and his men began to move. Boats were waiting for Washington's contingent at McKonkey's Ferry, about nine miles above Trenton. The oarsmen, wrapped in heavy blue coats, were John Glover's skilled Marbleheaders, a remarkable corps of fishermen from Massachusetts who were more comfortable on water than on land.

Glover, a heavyset redhead, had led his men in performing the phenomenal evacuation of Long Island; now they would perform a similar feat in taking Washington's twenty-four hundred men across the Delaware, this time fighting a heavy storm and sub-zero temperatures.

The men stood stoically on the river banks, waiting their turn to cross. The sleet mixed with snow pelted their faces, dripped under their collars. Some had covered the firelocks of their muskets with rags, attempting to keep them dry for the battle. Others, having no rags-or no foresight-watched miserably as their muskets became useless burdens.

Ice floated down the river, smashing against the boats and threatening to dump the passengers into the river. Hour after long hour passed, rows of weary men shifting in place as they waited on both sides of the freezing water. Washington hoped to have the crossing completed by midnight, but the stormy weather and ice-choked river slowed the movement. It wasn't until four in the morning that the army was ready to march.

Washington crossed the Delaware River, a dangerous prelude to the attack on Trenton, New Jersey. It took most of the night for Washington to get his 2,400 men across the icy river.

Four hours earlier, an American Tory had stopped at the home of Colonel Rall's host. The Tory said he had a vitally important message for the Hessian commander. Rall refused to see him. Nothing of great importance could be happening out in that storm, nothing that could not wait until morning. The Tory, desperate to convey his message, wrote Rall a note that could have undone everything Washington had so painfully planned.

In substance it said, "The Americans are on the move, coming toward Trenton." A servant passed the note to Rall. He disdainfully stuck it into his pocket without even looking at it and returned to his wine.

While Washington was struggling across the Delaware, Cadwalader and Ewing, commanders of the support contingents, were holding back. Ewing briefly agonized about crossing the icy water, then shook his head and decided not to attempt it. The river was impassable, he said. Cadwalader at least made the attempt.

He successfully shipped men across for several hours, but when he tried to transport the heavy cannon, the riverbanks were too slick, too perilously coated with ice. Some of the cannon slid out of control and disappeared into the water. He finally recalled his men and canceled the march.

A Bloodstained March

With one lone contingent left for the attack-but unaware of Cadwalader's and Ewing's failure-General Washington organized his men into two divisions and began to march. John Sullivan's division was to march along the river and attack the town from below. Nathanael Greene's division, which Washington accompanied, was to enter the town from above.

The men had a nine-mile march ahead of them, traveling slick, icy roads. Lowering their heads and pulling their wraps tight against the storm that whipped about them, the men forged ahead. One officer scribbled in his journal, "It is fearfully cold and raw and a snowstorm setting in. The wind...beats in the faces of the men. It will be a terrible night for the soldiers who have no shoes."

The officer's words proved to be sadly prophetic. Jagged ice on the road cut through worn-out shoes and threadbare stockings. The next day, Major James Wilkinson, coming behind, could follow their route by the bloodstains in the snow.

As the soldiers marched, a worried report came to Washington that the sleet was wetting their muskets. For some, even the precautionary rags were proving inadequate. Washington's determined reply: "Use the bayonet. I am resolved to take Trenton."

Victory at Trenton

Shortly after daybreak, about eight o'clock, the two columns converged on the town. Shocked Hessians had no time to prepare. Rall hurriedly dressed and formed a regiment on King Street. Another regiment, wearing scarlet uniforms, formed on the parallel Queen Street. The American artillery was waiting for them. Both armies hesitated, and time seemed to stand still. Then the gunners, under a slender young American officer named Alexander Hamilton, lit the touchholes of the cannon. Grapeshot roared from the cannons' mouths and the screaming Hessians fell back.

George Washington at Trenton. The Americans took the Hessian army at Trenton by surprise and won a significant victory.

On Queen Street the Hessians rolled out their own cannon and fired back. Bayonets at ready, a troop of Virginians sprinted toward the enemy, racing straight at the cannon.

Captain William Washington, cousin of the commander in chief, and Lieutenant James Monroe courageously led the charge.

In only moments the Americans had captured the cannon-but both Captain Washington and Lieutenant Monroe had fallen with serious wounds. Monroe likely would have bled to death had a doctor not been present. Through the doctor's careful ministerings, Monroe survived to become the fifth President of the United States.

Sullivan's men fought their way across town to meet Greene's group. Their muskets generally useless because of wet firelocks, the untrained, awkward Americans were forced to rely on the bayonet. Frustrated, some wisely crept into houses and stores and dried their firelocks. When Rall formed a counterattack they were ready, dropping the Hessian commander from his horse with two well-aimed slugs.

It was a glorious and almost unbelievable victory for the beleaguered American commander and his troops. Nearly 1,000 Hessians were taken captive; another 115 were killed or wounded. Four Americans had been wounded, but not a single one was lost in battle-although in the fierce night before, two had tragically frozen to death.

"The enemy have fled before us in the greatest panic that ever was known," one of the patriot soldiers wrote after the victory.

"Never were men in higher spirits than our whole army is."

Washington wrote August 20, 1778:

> The Hand of Providence has been so conspicuous in all this - the course of the war - that he must be worse than an infidel that lacks faith, and more wicked that has not gratitude to acknowledge his obligations; but it will be time enough for me to turn Preacher when my present appointment ceases.

General Washington wrote from Newport, Rhode Island, to William Gordon, March 9, 1781:

> We have, as you very justly observe, abundant reasons to thank Providence for its many favorable interpositions in our behalf. It has at times been my only dependence, for all other resources seemed to have failed us.

IN THE YEAR 1776 AD
PRISONERS OF WAR

The book, *The Real George Washington-The Man Who United America*, by Jay A. Parry and Andrew M. Allison, described the fate of captured American prisoners during the Revolutionary War:

> During the eight years of war, sixty thousand American soldiers died from

disease, exposure, or malnutrition. It is a marvel that so many survived.

Those who escaped death and the hospitals were at risk of being captured. The British captured some ten thousand men after major battles; the Americans captured about fifteen thousand. But neither side was prepared to hold prisoners of war. What could be done with all the captives?

The Americans handled the problem by setting large numbers loose on parole or exchanging them for patriot prisoners. The British, on the other hand, transformed churches and warehouses and barracks into prisons. When those became overcrowded, the redcoats began to place their captives in prison ships. In theory, they thought, the ships would be cleaner and more secure against escape. In reality they were neither. The ships were far too crowded to be clean. And any soldier who could swim-and who was not too weakened by fatigue, disease, malnutrition, and abuse-could often find a means of escape.

The prison ships soon became evil death ships. The British were not intentionally seeking to be cruel, but they killed more Americans through their flawed prison system than they did on the battlefield: between eight and ten thousand Americans died in the stench and disease of the prison ships anchored in the Hudson off New York City.

The diary of one soldier provides a stark description of the circumstances on board the transport Grosvenor. He was put on the ship on December 2, 1776, with about five hundred other men:

Friday, 13th of December 1776. We drawed bisd [bisquits?] and butter. A little water broth. We now see nothing but the mercy of God to intercede for us. Sorrowful times, all faces look pale, discouraged, discouraged.

Saturday, 14th. We drawed bisd. Times look dark. Deaths prevail among us...At night suffer cold and hunger. Nights very long and tiresome, weakness prevails.

Sunday, 15th. Drawed bisd. Paleness attends all faces. The melancholiest day I ever saw. At noon drawed meat and peas. Sunday gone and comfort. As sorrowful times as I ever saw.

Monday, 16th of December 1776 Sorrow increases. The tender mercies of men are cruelty.

Tuesday, 17th. Drawed bisd. At noon meat and rice. No fire. Suffer with cold and hunger. We are treated worse than cattle and hogs...

Sunday, 22nd. Last night nothing but groans all night of sick and dying. Men amazing to behold. Such hardness, sickness prevails fast. Deaths multiply. Drawed bisd. At noon meat and peas. Weather cold. Sunday gone and no comfort. Had nothing but sorrow and sadness. All faces sad.

Monday, 23rd. Drawed bisd and butter...About 20 gone from here today that enlisted in the king's service. [These were deserters who accepted the offer to escape the horrible conditions by changing allegiances, a not uncommon practice.] Times look very dark. But we are in hopes of an exchange. One dies almost every day...

Wednesday, 25th. [Christmas Day] Last night was a sorrowful night. Nothing but groans and cries all night...Sad times.

IN THE YEAR 1777 AD
BATTLE OF PRINCETON

𝔉rederick the Great of Prussia called the ten days between the Battle of Trenton, December 25, 1776, and the Battle of Princeton, January 3, 1777, "the most brilliant in the world's history."

After winning the Battle of Trenton, Christmas night, George Washington's small force met General Cornwallis' 8,000 man British army.

The night before the battle, Washington left his campfires burning and silently marched his army around the back of the British camp at Princeton, New Jersey.

At daybreak, January 3, 1777, Washington attacked, capturing three regiments of British troops. Enthusiasm swept America.

Yale President Ezra Stiles stated in an Election Address in 1783 before the Governor and General Assembly of Connecticut:

> In our lowest and most dangerous state, in 1776 and 1777, we sustained ourselves against the British Army of 60,000 troops, commanded by...the ablest generals Britain could procure throughout Europe, with a naval force of 22,000 seamen in above 80 men-of-war.
>
> Who but a Washington, inspired by Heaven, could have conceived the surprise move upon the enemy at Princeton-or that Christmas eve when Washington and his army crossed the Delaware? The United States are under peculiar obligations to become a holy people unto the Lord our God."

IN THE YEAR 1777 AD
VALLEY FORGE

Driven into Pennsylvania by the British, the Continental Army set up camp at Valley Forge, December 19, 1777, just 25 miles from British occupied Philadelphia. Lacking food and supplies, soldiers died at the rate of twelve per day. Of 11,000 soldiers, 2,500 died of cold, hunger and disease.

A Committee from Congress reported "feet and legs froze till they became black, and it was often necessary to amputate them."

Soldiers were there from every State in the new union, some as young as 12, others as old as 60, and though most were white, some were African American and American Indians. Quaker farmer Isaac Potts observed General Washington kneeling in prayer in the snow. Hessian Major Carl Leopold Baurmeister noted the only thing that kept the American army from disintegrating was their "spirit of liberty."

The book, *The Real George Washington-The Man Who United America*, by Jay A. Parry and Andrew M. Allison, describes General George Washington's troops at Valley Forge:

NO CLOTHES, NO SHOES, NO BLANKETS, NO SHELTER

The winter was well designed for a work of brutal destruction, nearly crushing the American army through intense starvation and cold. Washington grieved at the terrible hardship of his troops, but locating them at Valley Forge was a strategic necessity. Valley Forge, a wooded region south of the Schuylkill River, was only eighteen miles northwest of British-occupied Philadelphia. Washington was therefore close enough to keep an eye on the British while still being far enough to forestall a surprise attack.

Furthermore, with the American army there, British raiding parties could not as easily rove about seeking food and supplies, nor could they make a major march of any kind. As for the security of the American forces, Washington knew his troops would be safe at Valley Forge: the windy hills of the area provided terrain that could easily be defended.

As they began their stay there, the men lived in cold, drafty tents. In the weeks that followed they gradually built huts, fourteen feet wide by sixteen feet long, each housing twelve men. The huts, ready by mid-January, were crowded-but the number of men in each one contributed much-welcomed body warmth.

Washington voiced high praise for his ragamuffin army when he wrote to John Banister:

No history now extant can furnish an instance of an army's suffering such uncommon hardships as ours has done.

To see men without clothes to cover their nakedness, without blankets to lie on, without shoes (for the want of which their marches might be traced by the blood from their feet), and almost as often without provisions as with them, marching through the frost and snow, and at Christmas taking up their winter quarters within a day's march from the enemy, without a house or hut to cover them till they could be built, and submitting to it without a murmur, is a proof of patience and obedience which in my opinion can scarce be paralleled.

IN THE YEAR 1777
CAPTAIN COOK & CHRISTMAS ISLAND

British Captain James Cook (October 27, 1728-February 14, 1779) made three voyages to the Pacific Ocean, 1768-71, 1772-75, 1776-79, sailing from the Antarctic to the Bering Strait, from the coasts of North America to New Zealand and Australia.

Captain Cook was known for not allowing profanity on board, he required his men to wear clean clothes on Sunday and on occasions he conducted divine service for his crew.

Cook's wife gave him a Prayer Book, which he seems to have read in order, as he named a number of places discovered on significant day, such as the Whitsundays, Trinity Bay, Pentecost Islands and discovering the largest atoll in the Pacific Ocean on Christmas Day, 1777, Captain Cook named it "Christmas Island."

During World War II, American forces built a strategic airfield there.

IN THE YEAR 1783 AD
GENERAL WASHINGTON RESIGNED

On December 23, 1783, General George Washington resigned his commission to Congress; two days later he and Martha celebrated Christmas at Mount Vernon for the first time in nine years (age 51). The book, *The Real George Washington-The Man Who United America*, by Jay

A. Parry and Andrew M. Allison, describes General George Washington's resignation:

"THIS LAST SOLEMN ACT OF MY OFFICIAL LIFE"

On the twenty-third, exactly at noon, he presented himself at the door of the congressional chamber of the Maryland State House. The nineteen or twenty Congressmen who remained at the session sat soberly in their places with their hats on. After Washington was escorted into the room, the doors of the chamber were opened and leading Maryland citizens were allowed to enter. They soon filled the gallery to overflowing.

Washington resigned his commission to Congress, December 1783. The active fighting had ceased some two years before, and the peace treaty had been signed for months, but Washington remained on duty until the British finally departed America's shores. Secretary of Congress Charles Thomson ordered silence, and an expectant hush filled the room. President Thomas Mifflin then addressed Washington:

"Sir, the United States in Congress assembled are prepared to receive your communications."

Washington stood and bowed with dignity toward the members of Congress. The Congressmen responded by lifting their hats.

He drew from his pocket his prepared resignation speech and held it in front of him. His hand shook, and his voice trembled slightly. It was only with effort that he was able to begin.

"Mr. President: The great events on which my resignation depended having at length taken place, I have now the honor of...presenting myself before [Congress] to surrender into their hands the trust committed to me, and to claim the indulgence of retiring from the service of my country.

"Happy in the confirmation of our independence and sovereignty and pleased with the opportunity afforded the United States of becoming a respectable nation, I resign with satisfaction the appointment I accepted with diffidence-a diffidence in my abilities to accomplish so arduous a task, which, however, was superseded by a confidence in the rectitude of our cause, the support of the supreme power of the union, and the patronage of Heaven.

"The successful termination of the war has verified the most sanguine expectations, and my gratitude for the interposition of Providence, and [for] the assurance I have received from my countrymen, increases with every review of the momentous contest."

The General then spoke of his deep appreciation for the officers who had served with him, but his emotions welled up inside him and he found it difficult to continue. Finally, holding the paper with both hands to steady it, he was able to read on.

"I consider it an indispensable duty to close this last solemn act of my official life by commending the interests of our dearest country to the protection of Almighty God, and those who have the superintendence of them, to his holy keeping."

He was scarcely able to complete the sentence-his throat tightened and tears came brimming to the surface. As Congressman James McHenry, recalled, "His voice faltered and sank, and the whole house felt his agitations." The feeling in the room was so intense that "the spectators all wept, and there was hardly a member of Congress who did not drop tears."

After a pause Washington regained control. "Having now finished the work assigned me, I retire from the great theatre of action; and bidding an affectionate farewell to this august body under whose orders I have so long acted, I here offer my commission and take my leave of all the employments of public life."

Mifflin replied with a brief speech of his own, complimenting Washington on his superb leadership and his marked respect for civil authority. When the ceremony was completed, Washington bowed once again, then turned and walked from the chamber.

Congress adjourned moments later. With the formalities over, Washington reentered the room and shook hands with each of the delegates, bidding them a bittersweet farewell.

The Hearth and Home

His horse was waiting outside the building. Washington and his companions set off immediately, pressing on toward Mount Vernon. They doubtless spent the night in some tavern along the way.

The next morning, December 24, Washington rode rapidly past the gates of Maryland friends by whose fireside he would in other circumstances have been delighted to linger for an hour. Home was the magnet that drew him, home the haven he sought, home the years'-long dream that now was near fulfillment.

Every delay was a vexation and every halt a denial. At last the cold, clear waters of the Potomac came in sight, then the ferry and after that the blusterous passage, the last swift stage of the ride, the beloved trees, the yard, the doorway, Martha's embrace and the shrill, excited voices of "Jack" Custis's younger children-all this a richer reward than the addresses of cities, the salute of cannon and the approving words of the President of Congress.

He had arrived home barely in time for Christmas dinner with Martha and the grandchildren.

Despite his inability to find time for personal reading, Washington's deep interest in education continued. During his later years he saw to the education (and support) of twenty-two nieces and nephews. He donated £1,000 to an academy in Alexandria. He also contributed to other charitable causes, and virtually every Christmas he anonymously donated several hundred dollars to the poor.

IN THE YEAR 1804 AD
LEWIS & CLARK

Thomas Jefferson approved the Louisiana Purchase and commissioned the Lewis and Clark Expedition in 1803. President Thomas Jefferson explained their mission in a message to Congress, February 19, 1806:

In pursuance of a measure proposed to Congress by a message of January 18, 1803, and sanctioned by their approbation for carrying it into execution, Captain Meriwether Lewis, of the First Regiment of infantry, was appointed, with a party of men, to explore the river Missouri from its mouth to its source, and, crossing the highlands by the shortest portage, to seek the best water communication thence to the Pacific Ocean; and Lieutenant Clark was appointed second in command.

The book, *First Across the Continent-The Story of The Exploring Expedition of Lewis and Clark in 1804-6*, by Noah Brooks, describes Lewis and Clark's experiences on Christmas:

> ...One cold December day, a Mandan chief invited the explorers to join them in a grand buffalo hunt. The journal adds:-

> The weather now became excessively cold, the mercury often going thirty-two degrees below zero. Notwithstanding this, however, the Indians kept up their outdoor sports, one favorite game of which resembled billiards. But instead of a table, the players had an open flooring, about fifty yards long, and the balls were rings of stone, shot along the flooring by means of sticks like billiard-cues.

> The white men had their sports, and they forbade the Indians to visit them on Christmas Day, as this was one of their "great medicine days." The American flag was hoisted on the fort and saluted with a volley of musketry. The men danced among themselves; their best provisions were brought out and "the day passed," says the journal, "in great festivity."

> ...But, although their surroundings were not of a sort to make one very jolly, when Christmas came they observed the day as well as they could.

Here is what the journal says of the holiday:-

"We were awaked at daylight by a discharge of firearms, which was followed by a song from the men, as a compliment to us on the return of Christmas, which we have always been accustomed to observe as a day of rejoicing. After breakfast we divided our remaining stock of tobacco, which amounted to twelve carrots [hands], into two parts; one of which we distributed among such of the party as make use of it, making a present of a handkerchief to the others.

The remainder of the day was passed in good spirits, though there was nothing in our situation to excite much gayety. The rain confined us to the house, and our only luxuries in honor of the season were some poor elk, so much spoiled that we ate it through sheer necessity, a few roots, and some spoiled pounded fish.

"The next day brought a continuation of rain, accompanied with thunder, and a high wind from the southeast. We were therefore obliged to still remain in our huts, and endeavored to dry our wet articles before the fire. The fleas, which annoyed us near the portage of the Great Falls, have taken such possession of our clothes that we are obliged to have a regular search every day through our blankets as a necessary preliminary to sleeping at night.

These animals, indeed, are so numerous that they are almost a calamity to the Indians of this country. When they have once obtained the mastery of any house it is impossible to expel them, and the Indians have frequently different houses, to which they resort occasionally when the fleas have rendered their permanent residence intolerable; yet, in spite of these precautions, every Indian is constantly attended by multitudes of them, and no one comes into our house without leaving behind him swarms of these tormenting insects."

IN THE YEAR 1805 AD CHRISTMAS IN OREGON

"Ocian in view! O! the joy," wrote William Clark in his Journal, but the next day, November 8, 1805, Lewis and Clark realized they were only at Gray's Bay, still 20 miles from the Pacific. Clark wrote:

We found the swells or waves so high that we thought it imprudent to proceed...The seas rolled and tossed the canoes in such a manner this evening that several of our party were sea sick.

Pinned down by drenching, cold storms for 3 weeks, Lewis and Clark let the expedition decide where to build winter camp, even allowing Clark's slave, York, and the woman Indian guide, Sacagawea, to vote. A humble Christmas was celebrated in their new Fort Clatsop, near present-day Astoria, Oregon.

By Clark's estimate, their journey, commissioned by President Thomas Jefferson, had taken them 4,162 miles from the mouth of the Missouri River. Three months earlier, Meriwether Lewis, along with three companions, George Drouillard, Private John Shields and Private Hugh McNeal, reached the headwaters of the Missouri. Lewis recorded:

> The road took us to the most distant fountain of the waters of the Mighty Missouri...Private McNeal had exultingly stood with a foot on each side of this little rivulet and thanked his God that he had lived to bestride the mighty and heretofore deemed endless Missouri.

IN THE YEAR 1806 AD
LEWIS & CLARK, NEW YEAR'S DAY

The book, *First Across the Continent-The Story of The Exploring Expedition of Lewis and Clark in 1804-6*, by Noah Brooks, describes Lewis and Clark's experiences on Christmas:

> January 1, 1806. We were awaked at an early hour by the discharge of a volley of small arms, to salute the new year. This was the only mode of commemorating the day which our situation permitted; for, though we had reason to be gayer than we were at Christmas, our only dainties were boiled elk

and wappatoo, enlivened by draughts of pure water.

We were visited by a few Clatsops, who came by water, bringing roots and berries for sale.

Among this nation we observed a man about twenty-five years old, of a much lighter complexion than the Indians generally: his face was even freckled, and his hair long, and of a colour inclining to red. He was in habits and manners perfectly Indian; but, though he did not speak a word of English, he seemed to understand more than the others of his party; and, as we could obtain no account of his origin, we concluded that one of his parents, at least, must have been white.

IN THE YEAR 1818 AD ST. NICHOLAS CHURCH & "SILENT NIGHT"

At St. Nicholas Church in Oberndorf bei Salzburg, Austria, December 24, 1818, was first performed the song Silent Night. Originally in the German language as "Stille Nacht," it was written by the priest Father Joseph Mohr and the melody was composed by the Austrian headmaster Franz Xaver Gruber.

A story is that the church organ was not working, so the song was composed to be accompanied by a guitar for the Christmas service. The carol has been translated into over 44 languages, being translated into English in 1859 by

238

John Freeman Young, the second Bishop, Episcopal Diocese of Florida.

During the Christmas truce of 1914 in World War I, the song was sung simultaneously in French, English and German by troops as it was one of the few carols that soldiers on both sides of the front line knew.

> Silent night, holy night,
> All is calm, all is bright
> Round yon virgin mother and child.
> Holy infant so tender and mild,
> Sleep in heavenly peace,
> Sleep in heavenly peace.
>
> Silent night, holy night,
> Shepherds quake at the sight,
> Glories stream from heaven afar,
> Heavenly hosts sing alleluia;
> Christ the Savior, is born,
> Christ the Savior, is born.
>
> Silent night, holy night,
> Son of God, love's pure light
> Radiant beams from thy holy face,
> With the dawn of redeeming grace,
> Jesus, Lord, at thy birth,
> Jesus, Lord, at thy birth.

IN THE YEAR 1820
MISTLETOE, YULE LOG & HOLLY

𝔐istletoe - Washington Irving recorded northern European and Colonial American Christmas traditions in his *The Sketch Book of Geoffrey Crayon*, 1820.

According to ancient Christmas customs of Scandinavians, Celts and Teutons, a man and a woman who meet under a hanging of mistletoe were obliged to kiss. Washington Irving wrote:

> The mistletoe is still hung up in farm-houses and kitchens at Christmas, and the young men have the privilege of kissing the girls under it, plucking each time a berry from the bush. When the berries are all plucked the privilege ceases.

𝔜ule Log - The "Yule Log," was blessed by the Druids with a great ceremony at their winter feast, promising it would bring good luck if it could be kept burning during the entire winter solstice; an unburnt portion of the log was kept to begin the fire the following year and the ashes of it were thought to bring fertility to the soil.

Washington Irving wrote in his collection of stories, titled *Old Christmas,* 1820:

> The Yule-log is a great log of wood, sometimes the root of a tree, brought into the house with great ceremony, on Christmas eve, laid in the fireplace, and lighted with the brand of last year's clog.
>
> While it lasted there was great drinking, singing, and telling of tales. Sometimes it was accompanied by Christmas candles, but in the cottages the only light was

from the ruddy blaze of the great wood fire. The Yule-log was to burn all night; if it went out, it was considered a sign of ill luck.

𝕳olly - The name "Holly" is derived from the word "Holy," as it was used to decorate homes and churches during the Holy-Days. Washington Irving wrote in *The Sketch Book of Geoffrey Crayon, Gent.*, 1820:

> Even the poorest cottage welcomed the festive season with green decorations of bay and holly—the cheerful fire glanced its rays through the lattice, inviting the passenger to raise the latch, and join the gossip knot huddled around the hearth, beguiling the long evening with legendary jokes and oft-told Christmas tales...

> The housewives were stirring briskly about, putting their dwellings in order; and the glossy branches of holly, with their bright red berries, began to appear at the windows. The scene brought to mind an old writer's account of Christmas preparations:—"Now capons and hens, besides turkeys, geese, and ducks, with beef and mutton—must all die; for in twelve days a multitude of people will not be fed with a little.

> Now plums and spice, sugar and honey, square it among pies and broth. Now or never must music be in tune, for the youth must

dance and sing to get them a heat, while the aged sit by the fire. The country maid leaves half her market, and must be sent again, if she forgets a pack of cards on Christmas eve. Great is the contention of Holly and Ivy, whether master or dame wears the breeches...

Supper was announced shortly after our arrival. It was served up in a spacious oaken chamber, the panels of which shone with wax, and around which were several family portraits decorated with holly and ivy. Beside the accustomed lights, two great wax tapers, called Christmas candles, wreathed with greens, were placed on a highly-polished buffet among the family plate...

The Christmas Dinner
Lo, now is come the joyful'st feast!
Let every man be jolly,
Eache roome with yvie leaves is drest,
And every post with holly.
Now all our neighbours'
chimneys smoke,
And Christmas blocks are burning;
Their ovens they with bak't
meats choke,
And all their spits are turning.
Without the door let sorrow lie,
And if, for cold, it hap to die,
We'll bury't in a Christmas pye,
And evermore be merry.
—WITHERS'S Juvenilia.

...The dinner was served up in the great hall, where the Squire always held his Christmas banquet. A blazing, crackling fire of logs had been heaped on to warm the spacious apartment, and the flame went sparkling and wreathing up the wide-mouthed chimney.

The great picture of the crusader and his white horse had been profusely decorated with greens for the occasion; and holly and ivy had likewise been wreathed around the helmet and weapons on the opposite wall, which I understood were the arms of the same warrior...

The residence of people of fortune and refinement in the country, has diffused a degree of taste and elegance in rural economy that descends to the lowest class. The very laborer, with his thatched cottage and narrow slip of ground, attends to their embellishment.

The trim hedge, the grass-plot before the door, the little flower-bed bordered with snug box, the woodbine trained up against the wall, and hanging its blossoms about the lattice; the pot of flowers in the window; the holly, providently planted about the house, to cheat winter of its dreariness, and to throw in a semblance of green summer to cheer the fireside; all these bespeak the influence of taste, flowing down from high sources, and pervading the lowest levels of the public mind.

If ever Love, as poets sing, delights to visit a cottage, it must be the cottage of an English peasant.

The holly and the ivy,
Now both are full well grown.
Of all the trees that are in the wood,
The holly bears the crown.

(Chorus)
Oh, the rising of the sun,
The running of the deer.
The playing of the merry organ,
Sweet singing in the choir.

The holly bears a blossom
As white as lily flower;
And Mary bore sweet Jesus Christ
To be our sweet Savior. (Chorus)

The holly bears a berry
As red as any blood;
And Mary bore sweet Jesus Christ
To do poor sinners good. (Chorus)

The holly bears a prickle
As sharp as any thorn;
And Mary bore sweet Jesus Christ
On Christmas day in the morn. (Chorus)

The holly bears a bark
As bitter as any gall;
And Mary bore sweet Jesus Christ
For to redeem us all. (Chorus)

The holly and the ivy,
When they are both full grown,
Of all the trees that are in the wood,
The holly bears the crown. (Chorus)

IN THE YEAR 1829 AD
POINSETTIA

Christmas traditions started early on in United States history. One such began in 1829, when the first U.S. Ambassador to Mexico brought back from that country the "Flower of the Holy Night, which supposedly sprang up as a poor boy knelt to worship Jesus.

He planted them in South Carolina, and they grew in popularity throughout America. The U.S. Ambassador to Mexico's name was Dr. Joel Robert Poinsett, resulting in the flower being named "Poinsettia."

IN THE YEAR 1829 AD
JEDEDIAH SMITH

Jedediah Strong Smith (June 24, 1798-May 27, 1831), was an American trader and explorer. His expeditions were exceeded in importance only by those of Lewis and Clark. He helped lead expeditions up the Missouri River, with characters such as keelboatmen Mike Fink, Talbot, and Carpenter.

He led expeditions across the Rocky Mountains, 1822-26; from California to the Oregon coast; across the Mojave desert and the Sierra Nevadas; and along the Santa

Fe Trail, 1826-29. Jedediah Strong Smith, along with two other partners, operated the successful fur-trading company of Smith, Jackson and Sublette, in Salt Lake City.

Jedediah Strong Smith, who discovered the South Pass through the Rockies and established the first land route to California, noted in his journal:

> Then let us come forward with faith, nothing doubting, and He will most unquestionably hear us.

To his parents in Ohio, Jedediah Smith wrote on **Christmas Eve**, December 24, 1829, from Wind River on the east side of the Rocky Mountains:

> It is a long time since I left home & many times I have been ready, to bring my business to a close & endeavor to come home; but have been hindered hitherto...
>
> However I will endeavor, by the assistance of Divine Providence, to come home as soon as possible...but whether I shall ever be allowed the privilege, God only knows. I feel the need of the watch & care of a Christian Church.
>
> You may well suppose that our Society is of the roughest kind. Men of good morals seldom enter into business of this kind-I hope you will remember me before the Throne of Grace...

May God in His infinite mercy allow me soon to join My Parents is the Prayer of your undutiful Son, Jedediah S. Smith.

To his brother, Ralph Smith, Jedediah Smith wrote on **Christmas Eve**, December 24, 1829:

> I have passed through the Country from St. Louis, Missouri, to the North Paciffick Ocean, in different ways-through countrys of Barrenness & seldom one of the reverse, many Hostile Tribes of Indians inhabit this Space, and we are under the necessity of keeping a constant watch; notwithstanding our vigilance, we sometimes suffer;
>
> In Augt. 1827 ten Men, who were in company with me, lost their lives, by the Amuchabas Indians, on the Colorado River; & in July 1828 fifteen men, who were in Company with me lost their lives, by the Umpquah Indians, on the River of the Same name, it enters the North Paciffic, one hundred miles South of the Mouth of the Columbia-many others have lost their lives in different parts of the Country.
>
> My Brother believe me, we have Many dangers to face & many difficulties to encounter, but if I am Spared I am not anxious with regard to difficulties-for particulars you must await a meeting...
>
> As it respects my Spiritual welfare, I hardly durst Speak, I find myself one of the most ungrateful; unthankful, Creatures

imaginable. Oh when Shall I be under the care of a Christian Church? I have need of your Prayers, I wish our Society to bear me up before the Throne of Grace...I remain as ever your affectionate Brother, Jedediah Smith.

IN THE YEAR 1833 AD "BARN JESUS"

Hans Christian Andersen (April 2, 1805-August 4, 1875), was a Danish novelist and story-writer. He authored many fairy tales, including *The Ugly Duckling, The Emperor's New Clothes* and *The Tinder Box*. Hans Christian Andersen wrote what has become one of Denmark's best-known carols, entitled "Barn (Child) Jesus":

> Child Jesus came to earth this day,
> To save us sinners dying
> And cradled in the straw and hay
> The Holy One is lying.
> The star shines down the child to greet,
> The lowing oxen kiss his feet.
> Hallelujah, Hallelujah, Child Jesus!
> Take courage, Soul so weak and worn,
> Thy sorrows have departed.
> A Child in David's town is born,
> To heal the broken hearted.
> Then let us haste this child to find
> And children be in heart and mind.
> Hallelujah, Hallelujah, Child Jesus!

IN THE YEAR 1833 AD
"THE FIRST NOEL"

"The First Noel" was a traditional English carol, published in William B. Sandys's collection, *Christmas Carols, Ancient and Modern*, 1833.

> The First Noel, the Angels did say
> Was to certain poor shepherds in fields as they lay
> In fields where they lay keeping their sheep
> On a cold winter's night that was so deep.
> Noel, Noel, Noel, Noel
> Born is the King of Israel!
>
> They looked up and saw a star
> Shining in the East beyond them far
> And to the earth it gave great light
> And so it continued both day and night.
> Noel, Noel, Noel, Noel
> Born is the King of Israel!
>
> And by the light of that same star
> Three Wise men came from country far
> To seek for a King was their intent
> And to follow the star wherever it went.
> Noel, Noel, Noel, Noel
> Born is the King of Israel!
>
> This star drew nigh to the northwest
> O'er Bethlehem it took its rest
> And there it did both Pause and stay

Right o'er the place where Jesus lay.
Noel, Noel, Noel, Noel
Born is the King of Israel!

Then entered in those Wise men three
Full reverently upon their knee
And offered there in His presence
Their gold and myrrh and frankincense.
Noel, Noel, Noel, Noel
Born is the King of Israel!

Then let us all with one accord
Sing praises to our heavenly Lord
That hath made Heaven and earth of nought
And with his blood mankind has bought.
Noel, Noel, Noel, Noel
Born is the King of Israel!

IN THE YEAR 1835 AD
"O LITTLE TOWN OF BETHLEHEM"

Phillips Brooks, born December 13, 1835, was the bishop of the Episcopal Church in Massachusetts. He was taught at Harvard by Professors Henry Wadsworth Longfellow and Oliver Wendell Holmes. Phillips Brooks took a trip to the Holy Land in 1865, and wrote home:

> After an early dinner, we took our horses and rode to Bethlehem...It was only about two hours when we came to the town, situated on an eastern ridge of a range of hills,

surrounded by its terraced gardens. It is a good-looking town, better built than any other we have seen in Palestine...

Before dark, we rode out of town to the field where they say the shepherds saw the star.

It is a fenced piece of ground with a cave in it (all the Holy Places are caves here), in which, strangely enough, they put the shepherds.

The story is absurd, but somewhere in those fields we rode through the shepherds must have been...

As we passed, the shepherds were still 'keeping watch over their flocks or leading them home to fold.'

Upon his return to Massachusetts in September of 1866, Phillips Brooks wrote the carol, "O Little Town of Bethlehem."

O little town of Bethlehem!
How still we see thee lie;
Above thy deep and dreamless sleep,
The silent stars go by;
Yet in thy dark streets shineth,
The everlasting Light;
The hopes and fears
of all the years,
Are met in thee tonight.

IN THE YEAR 1842 AD "ANGELS WE HAVE HEARD ON HIGH"

"Angels We Have Heard on High" was a traditional French Christmas carol. Earliest known publication in Abbé Lambillotte's *Choix de cantiques sur des airs nouveaux,* 1842, though the words and tune may have existed from the 1700s:

> Angels we have heard on high
> Sweetly singing o'er the plains,
> And the mountains in reply
> Echoing their joyous strains.
>
> (Refrain)
> Gloria, in excelsis Deo!
> Gloria, in excelsis Deo!
>
> Shepherds, why this jubilee?
> Why your joyous strains prolong?
> What the gladsome tidings be
> Which inspire your heavenly song? (Refrain)
>
> Come to Bethlehem and see
> Christ Whose birth the angels sing;
> Come, adore on bended knee,
> Christ the Lord, the newborn King. (Refrain)
>
> See Him in a manger laid,
> Whom the choirs of angels praise;
> Mary, Joseph, lend your aid,
> While our hearts in love we raise. (Refrain)

252

IN THE YEAR 1842 AD
THE OREGON TRAIL

Dr. Marcus Whitman (September 4, 1802-November 29, 1847), was an American pioneer, doctor and missionary to the Indians in the Pacific Northwest. Dr. Marcus Whitman had practiced medicine for eight years in Rushville, New York, and in Canada before being appointed, in 1836, as a missionary-physician to Oregon, with his wife Narcissa, by the American Board of Foreign Missions. They set up missions at Wailatpu near Walla Walla, Washington, and at Laowai.

In the dead of winter, 1842-43, responding to a potential threat of closure, Dr. Marcus Whitman made a 4,000-mile trek east to persuade the Mission Board not to disband the mission. He also endeavored to interest the Government in settling the Oregon country and, in 1843, saw the first large wagon train head west on the Oregon Trail.

On July 3, 1923, just one month before his death, President Warren G. Harding delivered a speech in Meacham, Oregon, in remembrance of the Oregon Trail and the courageous missionaries to the Oregon and Washington territories. He unveiled a monument at Immigration Springs, and gave special recognition to the medical missionary Dr. Marcus Whitman, who, along with his wife, Narcissa, journeyed in 1836 to the Oregon territory.

Dr. Marcus Whitman was also honored by the United States government with a statue in the U.S. Capital Hall of Statuary for his key role in populating Oregon, which was vital in winning the boundary dispute with Great Britain, thereby bringing the territory under United States jurisdiction. President Warren G. Harding stated:

When I stood in that historic room in the White House and my imagination depicted the simple scene, I could not but feel that the magnificence of Marcus Whitman's glorious deed has yet to find adequate recognition in any form. Here was a man who, with a single companion, **in the dead of winter [1842],** struggled through pathless drifts and blinding storms, four thousand miles, with the sole aim to serve his country and his God.

Eighty years and eight months ago he was pushing grimly and painfully through this very pass on his way from Walla Walla to Fort Hall, thence, abandoning the established northern route as impassable, off to the South through unknown, untrodden lands, past the Great Salt Lake, to Santa Fe, then hurriedly on to St. Louis and finally, after a few days, again on the home-stretch to his destination, taking as many months as it now takes days to go from Walla Walla to Washington.

It was more than a desperate and perilous trip that Marcus Whitman undertook. It was a race against time. Public opinion was rapidly crystallizing into a judgment that the Oregon country was not worth claiming, much less worth fighting for; that, even though it could be acquired against the insistence of Great Britain, it would prove to be a liability rather than an asset.

It is with sheer amazement that we now read the declarations of leading men of that period. So good an American, so sturdy a frontiersman, so willing a fighter, as General Jackson, shook his head ominously in fear lest the national domain should get too far outspread, and warned the country that its safety "lay in a compact government."

Senator McDuffie, of South Carolina, declared he "would not give a pinch of snuff for the whole territory," and expressed the wish that the Rocky Mountains were "an impassable barrier." Senator Dayton, of New Jersey, said that, with very limited exceptions, "the whole country was as irreclaimable and barren a waste as the Sahara desert," and that malaria had carried away most of its native population.

Even so far-seeing and staunch an advocate of western interests as Thomas Benton protested that the ridge of the Rockies should be made our western boundary, and avowed that "on the highest peak the statue of the fabled god, Terminus, should be erected, never to be thrown down."

Webster, although not definitely antagonistic, was uninterested and lukewarm. Years before he had pronounced Oregon "a barren, worthless country, fit only for wild beasts and wild men," and he was not one who changed opinions readily.

But neither was Whitman one easily dismayed. Encouraged by the manifest friendliness of President Tyler, he portrayed with vivid eloquence the salubrity of the climate, the fertility of the soil, the magnitude of the forests, the evidences of ore in the mountains, and the splendor of the wide valleys drained by the great rivers.

And he did not hesitate to speak plainly, as one who knew, even like the prophet Daniel. "Mr. Secretary," he declared, "you would better give all New England for the cod and mackerel fisheries of Newfoundland than to barter away Oregon."

Then turning to the President, he added quietly but beseechingly: "All I ask is that you will not barter away Oregon or allow English interference until I can lead a band of stalwart American settlers across the plains. For this I shall try to do!"

The manly appeal was irresistible. He sought only for the privilege of proving his faith. The just and considerate Tyler could not refuse.

"Doctor Whitman," he rejoined sympathetically, "your long ride and frozen limbs testify to your courage and your patriotism. Your credentials establish your character. Your request is granted!"...

Never in the history of the world has there been a finer example of civilization following Christianity. The missionaries led under the banner of the cross, and the settlers moved close behind under the star-spangled symbol of the nation.

IN THE YEAR 1843 AD
"A CHRISTMAS CAROL"

In 1843, Charles Dickens wrote *A Christmas Carol,* which sold 6,000 copies the first day. Perhaps the most touching line was Tiny Tim's "God bless us every one!"

> ...and it was always said of him, that he knew how to keep Christmas well, if any man alive possessed the knowledge. May that be truly said of us, and all of us! And so, as Tiny Tim observed, "God bless Us, Every One!"

In 1849, Charles Dickens wrote *The Life of Our Lord* for his ten children, depicting with biblical accuracy the birth, ministry, death and resurrection of Jesus Christ. Charles Dickens stated:

> The New Testament is the very best book that ever was or ever will be known in the world.

IN THE YEAR 1843 AD
CHRISTMAS CARDS

In 1843, J.C. Hardy made the first Lithographic Christmas Cards. These cards carried the Christmas message and were convenient to mail.

IN THE YEAR 1847 AD
"O HOLY NIGHT"

"Ⓞ Holy Night" ("Cantique de Noël") was composed by Adolphe Adam in 1847 to the French poem "Minuit, chrétiens" (Midnight, Christians) by Placide Cappeau (1808–1877), a wine merchant and poet, who had been asked by a parish priest to write a Christmas poem. John Sullivan Dwight, editor of *Dwight's Journal of Music*, created a singing edition based on Cappeau's French text in 1855.

O holy night! The stars are brightly shining,
It is the night of our dear Saviour's birth.
Long lay the world in sin and error pining,
'Til He appear'd and the soul felt its worth.

A thrill of hope the weary world rejoices,
For yonder breaks a new and glorious morn.
Fall on your knees! O hear the angels' voices!
O night divine, O night when Christ was born;
O night divine, O night, O night Divine.

Led by the light of Faith serenely beaming,
With glowing hearts by His cradle we stand.
So led by light of a star sweetly gleaming,
Here come the wise men from Orient land.

The King of Kings lay thus in lowly manger;
In all our trials born to be our friend.
He knows our need, to our weakness is no stranger,
Behold your King! Before Him lowly bend!
Behold your King, Before Him lowly bend!

Truly He taught us to love one another;
His law is love and His gospel is peace.
Chains shall He break for the slave is our brother;
And in His name all oppression shall cease.

Sweet hymns of joy in grateful chorus raise we,
Let all within us praise His holy name.
Christ is the Lord! O praise His Name forever,
His power and glory evermore proclaim.
His power and glory evermore proclaim.

IN THE YEAR 1850 AD
"IT CAME UPON A MIDNIGHT CLEAR"

Richard Storrs Willis (1819-1900) first published
"It Came Upon a Midnight Clear" in *Church Chorals and
Choir Studies*, New York, 1850.

It came upon the midnight clear,
That glorious song of old,
From angels bending near the earth,
To touch their harps of gold;
"Peace on the earth, good will to men,
From heaven's all gracious King."
The world in solemn stillness lay,
To hear the angels sing.

Still through the cloven skies they come,
With peaceful wings unfurl
And still their heavenly music floats,
O'er all the weary world.

Above its sad and lowly plains,
They bend on hovering wing
And ever o'er its Babel sounds,
The blessed angels sing.

Yet with the woes of sin and strife,
The world has suffered long;
Beneath the angel-strain have rolled,
Two thousand years of wrong;
And man, at war with man, hears not,
The love song which they bring:
O hush the noise, ye men of strife,
And hear the angels sing.

And ye, beneath life's crushing load,
Whose forms are bending low
Who toil along the climbing way
With painful steps and slow
Look now! for glad and golden hours
Come swiftly on the wing
O rest beside the weary road
And hear the angels sing.

For lo! the days are hastening on,
By prophet bards foretold,
When, with the ever-circling years,
Shall come the Age of Gold;
When peace shall over all the earth,
Its ancient splendors fling,
And all the world give back the song,
Which now the angels sing.

IN THE YEAR 1853 AD
"GOOD KING WENCESLAS"

𝕴n 1853, English hymnwriter John Mason Neale (1818-1866) wrote the "Wenceslas" lyrics. He had been ordained as a clergyman in 1842, was fluent in 20 languages, and translated many hymns from their original Greek and Latin tongues.

Many Christmas hymns were written or translated by him, including: "Jerusalem the Golden"; "The Day is Past and Over"; "Come, Ye Faithful"; and the favorite "Good King Wenceslas," in collaboration with his music editor Thomas Helmore. The carol was first published in *Carols for Christmas-Tide*, 1853.

Wenceslaus I was the Duke of Bohemia (907–935), who was martyred following his assassination by his brother Boleslaw on September 28, 935. He is considered the Patron Saint of the Czech Republic. He embodied the High Middle Ages concept of the rex justus, or "righteous king." The chronicler Cosmas of Prague, around the year 1119, wrote:

> But his deeds I think you know better than I could tell you; for, as is read in his Passion, no one doubts that, rising every night from his noble bed, with bare feet and only one chamberlain, he went around to God's churches and gave alms generously to widows, orphans, those in prison and afflicted by every difficulty, so much so that he was considered, not a prince, but the father of all the wretched.

Although Wenceslas was only a duke, Holy Roman Emperor Otto I posthumously conferred on him the title of king. Centuries later, emulating good King Wenceslas, Pope Pius II walked ten miles barefoot in the ice and snow as an act of pious thanksgiving.

The song is about Wenceslas going out to give alms to poor peasants on the cold winter's night of the Feast of Stephen (the second day of Christmas, December 26). Caught in the freezing weather, his page was about to give up the struggle against the cold weather, but the king told the young page to follow him by stepping in the footprints he left in the snow. Step by step, through the deep snow, the page was able to follow.

> Good King Wenceslas looked out
> On the feast of Stephen,
> When the snow lay round about,
> Deep and crisp and even;
> Brightly shone the moon that night,
> Though the frost was cruel,
> When a poor man came in sight,
> Gath'ring winter fuel.
>
> "Hither, page, and stand by me,
> If thou know'st it, telling,
> Yonder peasant, who is he?
> Where and what his dwelling?"
> "Sire, he lives a good league hence,
> Underneath the mountain;
> Right against the forest fence,
> By Saint Agnes' fountain."

"Bring me flesh, and bring me wine,
Bring me pine logs hither;
Thou and I will see him dine,
When we bear him thither."
Page and monarch forth they went,
Forth they went together,
Through the rude wind's wild lament,
And the bitter weather.

"Sire, the night is darker now,
And the wind blows stronger;
Fails my heart, I know not how,
I can go no longer."
"Mark my footsteps, my good page,
Tread thou in them boldly;
Thou shalt find the winter's rage,
Freeze thy blood less coldly."

In his master's steps he trod,
Where the snow lay dinted;
Heat was in the very sod,
Which the Saint had printed.
Therefore, Christian men, be sure,
Wealth or rank possessing,
Ye who now will bless the poor,
Shall yourselves find blessing.

IN THE YEAR 1856 AD
FIRST WHITE HOUSE CHRISTMAS TREE

President Franklin Pierce placed the first Christmas Tree in the White House.

IN THE YEAR 1857 AD
"WE THREE KINGS OF ORIENT ARE"

In 1857, Rev. John Henry Hopkings wrote "We three Kings of Orient are" for the Christmas pageant of the General Theological Seminary in New York City:

> We three kings of Orient are
> Bearing gifts we traverse afar
> Field and fountain, moor and mountain
> Following yonder star
>
> O Star of wonder, star of night
> Star with royal beauty bright
> Westward leading, still proceeding
> Guide us to thy Perfect Light
>
> Born a King on Bethlehem's plain
> Gold I bring to crown Him again
> King forever, ceasing never
> Over us all to rein
>
> O Star of wonder, star of night
> Star with royal beauty bright
> Westward leading, still proceeding
> Guide us to Thy perfect light
>
> Frankincense to offer have I
> Incense owns a Deity nigh
> Pray'r and praising, all men raising
> Worship Him, God most high

O Star of wonder, star of night
Star with royal beauty bright
Westward leading, still proceeding
Guide us to Thy perfect light

Myrrh is mine, its bitter perfume
Breathes of life of gathering gloom
Sorrowing, sighing, bleeding, dying
Sealed in the stone-cold tomb

O Star of wonder, star of night
Star with royal beauty bright
Westward leading, still proceeding
Guide us to Thy perfect light

Glorious now behold Him arise
King and God and Sacrifice
Alleluia, Alleluia
Earth to heav'n replies

O Star of wonder, star of night
Star with royal beauty bright
Westward leading, still proceeding
Guide us to Thy perfect light

IN THE YEAR 1860 AD
SOUTH CAROLINA SECEDED

In 1860, as President-elect, Lincoln received callers, such as Thurlow Weed in Springfield, Illinois, and dealt with cabinet issues, he was concerned that federal forts had been taken in the Southm and on December 20, 1860, he received news that South Carolina had seceded from the Union.

IN THE YEAR 1861 AD
LINCOLN AT CHRISTMAS SERVICE

In 1861, President Lincoln was deeply involved in Civil War problems such as the Trent affair, but found time on December 22, 1861, to attend services at New York Avenue Presbyterian Church. On Christmas morning he held an important Cabinet meeting, but was able to entertain a large number of dinner guests by evening.

IN THE YEAR 1862 AD
LINCOLN VISITED HOSPITALS

In 1862, President Lincoln again was absorbed with military matters and was preparing the final draft of the Emancipation Proclamation. On December 23, 1862, Lincoln wrote to Fanny McCullough, whose father had been killed in action and had been a long-time friend of his. Both President and Mrs. Lincoln visited soldiers in Washington hospitals on Christmas Day.

IN THE YEAR 1863 AD
EMANCIPATION PROCLAMATION

On January 1, 1863, the Emancipation Proclamation went into effect. President Lincoln reassured the Massachusetts Anti-Slavery Society he had no intention of retracting it. On Christmas Day he had discussed the constitutionality of the draft with John Hay, one of his private secretaries.

IN THE YEAR 1864 AD "I HEARD THE BELLS ON CHRISTMAS DAY"

Henry Wadsworth Longfellow's oldest son Charles Appleton Longfellow enlisted in the Union Army during the Civil War without Henry's knowledge, being informed by a letter from him dated March 14, 1863:

> I have tried hard to resist the temptation of going without your leave but I cannot any longer. I feel it to be my first duty to do what I can for my country and I would willingly lay down my life for it if it would be of any good.

Appointed as a lieutenant, Charles was severely wounded in November on 1864 at the Battle of New Hope Church in Virginia during the Mine Run Campaign. This occurred shortly after Henry Wadsworth Longfellow's wife, Frances, had died as result of an accidental fire.

On Christmas Day that year, 1864, Longfellow wrote his poem "Christmas Bells." It was published in February 1865 in *Our Young Folks*, a juvenile magazine published by Ticknor and Fields. In 1872 the poem was set to music by the English organist, John Baptiste Calkin, who used a melody he previously used in 1848.

> I Heard the Bells on Christmas Day
> Their old familiar carols play,
> And wild and sweet the words repeat
> Of peace on earth, good will to men.

I thought how, as the day had come,
The belfries of all Christendom
Had rolled along the unbroken song
Of peace on earth, good will to men.

And in despair I bowed my head:
"There is no peace on earth," I said,
"For hate is strong and mocks the song
Of peace on earth, good will to men."

Then pealed the bells more loud and deep:
"God is not dead, nor doth he sleep;
The wrong shall fail, the right prevail,
With peace on earth, good will to men."

Till, ringing singing, on its way,
The world revolved from night to day,
A voice, a chime, a chant sublime,
Of peace on earth, good will to men!

IN THE YEAR 1864 AD
SAVANNAH, GEORGIA

On December 25, 1864, President Lincoln received the following dispatch from General Sherman, who had captured Savannah, Georgia:

I beg to present you as a Christmas gift the city of Savannah with 150 heavy guns & plenty of ammunition & also about 25000 bales of cotton.

On December 26, 1864, Lincoln gave a Christmas reception at the White House.

IN THE YEAR 1865 AD
"GO, TELL IT ON THE MOUNTAIN"

"Go, Tell It on the Mountain" was a popular African-American spiritual song. It was included in a work compiled by John Wesley Work, Jr., in 1865, and has been sung and recorded by many gospel and secular performers, including Harry T. Burleigh in 1917:

> Go, tell it on the mountain,
> Over the hills and everywhere;
> Go, tell it on the mountain,
> That Jesus Christ is born.
>
> While shepherds kept their watching
> o'er silent flocks by night,
> Behold, throughout the heavens
> There shone a holy light.
>
> Go, tell it on the mountain,
> Over the hills and everywhere;
> Go, tell it on the mountain,
> That Jesus Christ is born.
>
> The shepherds feared and trembled,
> When lo! above the earth,
> Rang out the angels chorus
> That hailed our Savior's birth.

Go, tell it on the mountain,
Over the hills and everywhere;
Go, tell it on the mountain,
That Jesus Christ is born.

Down in a lowly manger
The humble Christ was born
And God sent us salvation
That blessed Christmas morn.

IN THE YEAR 1865 AD
"WHAT CHILD IS THIS"

In 1865, William Chatterton Dix wrote the Christmas carol, "What Child Is This":

What child is this, who, laid to rest
On Mary's lap, is sleeping?
Whom angels greet with anthems sweet,
While shepherds watch are keeping? (Chorus)

This, this is Christ the King,
Whom shepherds guard and angels sing:
Haste, haste to bring him laud,
The Babe, the Son of Mary!

Why lies he in such mean estate
Where ox and ass are feeding?
Good Christian, fear for sinners here,
The silent Word is pleading. (Chorus)

So bring Him incense, gold, and myrrh,
Come peasant king to own Him,
The King of kings, salvation brings,
Let loving hearts enthrone Him.

Raise, raise the song on high,
The Virgin sings her lullaby:
Joy, joy, for Christ is born,
The Babe, the Son of Mary!

IN THE YEAR 1868 AD
FULL PARDON & AMNESTY

On Christmas day, 1868, President Johnson proclaimed full pardon and amnesty for all who had participated in secession, without reserve or exception.

IN THE YEAR 1870 AD
CHRISTMAS DAY FEDERAL HOLIDAY

On June 28, 1870, President Ulysses S. Grant signed a Bill making Christmas Day a Federal Holiday.

IN THE YEAR 1885 AD
"AWAY IN A MANGER"

In 1885, "Away in a Manger" was published in a Lutheran Sunday school book. It was edited in 1892 by Charles H. Gabriel, and published in *Gabriel's Vineyard*

Songs (Louisville, Ky., Guide Printing & Publishing Company).
It was set to the music of William J. Kirkpatrick in 1895.

> Away in a manger,
> No crib for His bed
> The little Lord Jesus
> Laid down His sweet head
> The stars in the bright sky
> Looked down where He lay
> The little Lord Jesus
> Asleep on the hay
>
> The cattle are lowing
> The poor Baby wakes
> But little Lord Jesus
> No crying He makes
> I love Thee, Lord Jesus
> Look down from the sky
> And stay by my side,
> 'Til morning is nigh.
>
> Be near me, Lord Jesus,
> I ask Thee to stay
> Close by me forever
> And love me I pray
> Bless all the dear children
> In Thy tender care
> And take us to heaven
> To live with Thee there

IN THE YEAR 1893 AD
CHRISTMAS DAY NATIONAL HOLIDAY

Christmas Day was an official Holiday in all U.S. States and Territories.

IN THE YEAR 1904 AD
BOOKER T. WASHINGTON

Booker T. Washington mentioned Christmas in *Up From Slavery: An Autobiography*, 1904:

> My mother's husband, who was the stepfather of my brother John and myself, did not belong to the same owners as did my mother. In fact, he seldom came to our plantation. I remember seeing his there perhaps once a year, that being about Christmas time. In some way, during the war, by running away and following the Federal soldiers, it seems, he found his way into the new state of West Virginia.
>
> As soon as freedom was declared, he sent for my mother to come to the Kanawha Valley, in West Virginia. At that time a journey from Virginia over the mountains to West Virginia was rather a tedious and in some cases a painful undertaking. What little clothing and few household goods we had were placed in a cart, but the children walked the greater portion of the distance, which was several hundred miles...

The coming of Christmas, that first year of our residence in Alabama, gave us an opportunity to get a farther insight into the real life of the people. The first thing that reminded us that Christmas had arrived was the "foreday" visits of scores of children rapping at our doors, asking for "Chris'mus gifts! Chris'mus gifts!"

Between the hours of two o'clock and five o'clock in the morning I presume that we must have had a half-hundred such calls. This custom prevails throughout this portion of the South to-day. During the days of slavery it was a custom quite generally observed throughout all the Southern states to give the coloured people a week of holiday at Christmas...

In the school we made a special effort to teach our students the meaning of Christmas, and to give them lessons in its proper observance. In this we have been successful to a degree that makes me feel safe in saying that the season now has a new meaning, not only through all that immediate region, but, in a measure, wherever our graduates have gone.

At the present time one of the most satisfactory features of the Christmas and Thanksgiving season at Tuskegee is the unselfish and beautiful way in which our graduates and students spend their time in administering to the comfort and happiness of others, especially the unfortunate. Not long ago some of our young men spent a holiday in rebuilding a cabin for a helpless coloured women who was about seventy-five years old.

At another time I remember that I made it known in chapel, one night, that a very poor student was suffering from cold, because he needed a coat. The next morning two coats were sent to my office for him. I have referred to the disposition on the part of the white people in the town of Tuskegee and vicinity to help the school. From the first, I resolved to make the school a real part of the community in which it was located.

I was determined that no one should have the feeling that it was a foreign institution, dropped down in the midst of the people, for which they had no responsibility and in which they had no interest. I noticed that the very fact that they had been asking to contribute toward the purchase of the land made them begin to feel as if it was going to be their school, to a large degree.

I noted that just in proportion as we made the white people feel that the institution was a part of the life of the community, and that, while we wanted to make friends in Boston, for example, we also wanted to make white friends in Tuskegee, and that we wanted to make the school of real service to all the people, their attitude toward the school became favourable.

Perhaps I might add right here, what I hope to demonstrate later, that, so far as I know, the Tuskegee school at the present time has no warmer and more enthusiastic friends anywhere than it has among the white citizens of Tuskegee and throughout the state of Alabama and the entire South. From the first, I have advised our people in the South to make friends in every straightforward, manly way with their next-door neighbour, whether he be a black man or a white man...

When the Englishman takes you into his heart and friendship, he binds you there as with cords of steel, and I do not believe that there are many other friendships that are so lasting or so satisfactory. Perhaps I can illustrate this point in no better way than by relating the following incident.

Mrs. Washington and I were invited to attend a reception given by the Duke and Duchess of Sutherland, at Stafford House- said to be the finest house in London; I may add that I believe the Duchess of Sutherland is said to be the most beautiful woman in England. There must have been at least three hundred persons at this reception.

Twice during the evening the Duchess sought us out for a conversation, and she asked me to write her when we got home, and tell her more about the work at Tuskegee. This I did.

When Christmas came we were surprised and delighted to receive her photograph with her autograph on it. The correspondence has continued, and we now feel that in the Duchess of Sutherland we have one of our warmest friends.

IN THE YEAR 1906 AD
HELEN KELLER

In December of 1906, Helen Keller wrote in the *Ladies Home Journal*:

> The only real blind person at Christmastime is he who has not Christmas in his heart.

IN THE YEAR 1914 AD
CHRISTMAS TRUCE

On Christmas Eve, during the First World War, near Ypres in Belgium, there was an unofficial ceasefire. German and British troops, and some French, left their trenches and walked across no man's land to celebrate Christmas together. They recovered bodies, had joint burial services, and sang Christmas carols.

An Open Christmas Letter from 101 British women suffragists was addressed "To the Women of Germany and Austria" as the first Christmas of the war approached. Pope Benedict XV, on December 7, 1914, also begged for an truce, asking: "that the guns may fall silent at least upon the night the angels sang."

Though these requests were officially rebuffed, an estimated 100,000 British and German troops ceased fighting along the length of the Western Front.

It began on Christmas Eve, December 24, 1914, when German troops began decorating the area around their trenches, placing candles on their trenches and Christmas trees, then began singing Christmas carols.

The British responded by singing carols, and the two sides continued by shouting Christmas greetings to each other. Soon excursions were made across "No Man's Land" and small gifts were exchanged, such as food, tobacco, alcohol, and souvenirs such as buttons and hats.

The artillery in the region fell silent that night. Bruce Bairnsfather, who served during the war, wrote:

> I wouldn't have missed that unique and weird Christmas Day for anything...I spotted a German officer, some sort of lieutenant I should think, and being a bit of a collector, I intimated to him that I had taken a fancy to some of his buttons...
>
> I brought out my wire clippers and, with a few deft snips, removed a couple of his buttons and put them in my pocket. I then gave him two of mine in exchange...
>
> The last I saw was one of my machine gunners, who was a bit of an amateur hairdresser in civil life, cutting the unnaturally long hair of a docile Boche, who was patiently kneeling on the ground whilst the automatic clippers crept up the back of his neck.

General Sir Horace Smith-Dorrien, commander of the British II Corps, was irate when he heard what was happening, and issued strict orders forbidding friendly communication with the opposing German troops. Another person who opposed the truce was a young corporal in the 16th Bavarian Reserve Infantry by the name of Adolf Hitler.

IN THE YEAR 1918 AD
WOODROW WILSON & WWI

On December 8, 1918, in an appeal of support for the American Red Cross just a month after the fighting in World War I had ceased, President Woodrow Wilson stated:

> One year ago, twenty-two million Americans, by enrolling as members of the Red Cross at Christmas time, sent to the men who were fighting our battles overseas a stimulating message of cheer and good-will....Now, by God's grace, the Red Cross Christmas message of 1918 is to be a message of peace as well as a message of good-will.

On December 25, 1918, in an address delivered to General Pershing and the American troops stationed on the battle-front in France, President Woodrow Wilson stated:

> While it is hard far away from home, confidentially, to bid you a Merry Christmas, I can, I think, confidentially, promise you a

Happy New Year, and I can from the bottom of my heart say, God bless you.

IN THE YEAR 1932 AD HERBERT HOOVER

President Herbert Hoover wrote in 1932:

> Your CHRISTMAS Service held each year at the foot of a living tree which was alive at the time of the birth of Christ...should be continued as a further symbol of the unbroken chain of life leading back to this great moment in the spiritual life of mankind.

IN THE YEAR 1942 AD "I'M DREAMING OF A WHITE CHRISTMAS"

The son of a rabbi, Irving Berlin was born in Russia on May 11, 1888. He was four-years old when his family immigrated to New York. Falling in love with America, he served in the U.S. infantry during World War I and wrote some of the country's most popular songs, including: "Alexander's Ragtime Band," "White Christmas" and "God Bless America," the royalties from which he gave to the Boy Scouts and Girl Scouts.

In 1945, he received the Army's Medal of Merit from President Truman; in 1955, he received the Congressional Gold Medal from President Eisenhower, and in 1977, he received the Presidential Medal of Freedom from President Ford.

On October 12, 2001, Congressman Mike Castle of Delaware stated:

> In the aftermath of September 11...
> Republicans and Democrats burst into that
> song of the same name by Irving Berlin on
> the steps of the U.S. Capitol...It was a slogan
> for peace.

> God Bless America, Land that I Love,
> Stand Beside Her, and Guide Her,
> Through the Night, with the Light From Above.
> From the Mountains, to the Prairies,
> To the Oceans White with Foam,
> God Bless America, My Home Sweet Home,
> God Bless America, My Home Sweet Home!

Irving Berlin wrote the words and music for White Christmas in 1942 and the song was originally featured in the movie *Holiday Inn* starring Bing Crosby. It struck a chord with the soldiers fighting in the Second World War and their families waiting back home.

The song was recorded by Bing Crosby with John Scott Trotter's orchestra and the Ken Darby Singers. It became so popular that it was featured in the 1954 movie *White Christmas,* starring Bing Crosby, Danny Kaye, Vera-Ellen, and Rosemary Clooney, aunt of actor George Clooney and Carlos Campo, Regent University President.

> I'm dreaming of a white Christmas
> Just like the ones I used to know
> Where the treetops glisten,
> and children listen
> To hear sleigh bells in the snow

I'm dreaming of a white Christmas
With every Christmas card I write
May your days be merry and bright
And may all your Christmases be white

I'm dreaming of a white Christmas
With every Christmas card I write
May your days be merry and bright
And may all your Christmases be white

IN THE YEAR 1942 AD FRANKLIN D. ROOSEVELT

𝔍n his 1942 Christmas Address, President Franklin D. Roosevelt stated:

I say that loving our neighbor as we love ourselves is not enough- that we as a Nation and as individuals will please God best by showing regard for the laws of God. There is no better way of fostering good will toward man than by first fostering good will toward God. If we love Him we will keep His Commandments...

In sending Christmas greetings to the armed forces and merchant sailors...we include our pride in their bravery on the fighting fronts...It is significant that Christmas Day our plants and factories will be stilled. That is not true of the other holidays...

On all other holidays work goes on-gladly- for the winning of the war. So Christmas becomes the only holiday in all the year. I like to think that this is so because Christmas is a holy day. May all it stands for live and grow throughout the years.

IN THE YEAR 1944 AD BATTLE OF THE BULGE

The 101 Airborne had parachuted into southern Belgium, behind enemy lines. The Nazis, who had amassed three armies for an enormous attack against the Allies in the Ardennes Forest, had surrounded the 101st Airborne and was demanding their surrender.

U.S. General Anthony McAuliffe answered in one word: "Nuts." This response confused the Nazi commander, causing him to hesitate. Marching to the rescue was the U.S. Third Army, but it was hindered due to bad weather. General Patton directed Chaplain O'Neill to compose a prayer for his 250,000 troops to pray:

> Almighty and most merciful Father, we humbly beseech Thee, of Thy great goodness, to restrain these immoderate rains...Hearken to us as soldiers who call upon Thee...Establish Thy justice among men and nations."

On the back side of card was General Patton's Christmas Greeting to his army. The weather cleared and the Allies counterattacked. On December 22, 1944, during the historic "Battle of the Bulge," General Eisenhower declared in his "Orders of the Day":

By rushing out from his fixed defenses the enemy may give us the chance to turn his great gamble into his worst defeat. So I call upon every man, of all the Allies, to rise now to new heights of courage, of resolution and of effort. Let everyone hold before him a single thought-to destroy the enemy on the ground, in the air, everywhere-destroy him! United in this determination and with unshakable faith in the cause for which we fight, we will, with God's help, go forward to our greatest victory.

Two days later President Franklin Roosevelt stated:

It is not easy to say 'Merry Christmas' to you, my fellow Americans, in this time of destructive war...We will celebrate this Christmas Day in our traditional American way...because the teachings of Christ are fundamental in our lives...the story of the coming of the immortal Prince of Peace.

IN THE YEAR 1946 AD
HARRY S TRUMAN

On December 24, 1946, lighting the National Christmas Tree, President Truman said:

Our...hopes of future years turn to a little town in the hills of Judea where on a winter's night two thousand years ago the prophecy of Isaiah was fulfilled. Shepherds keeping watch by night over their flock heard the glad tidings of great joy from the angels of the Lord singing,

'Glory to God in the Highest and on Earth, peace, good will toward men.'...If we will accept it, the star of faith will guide us into the place of peace as it did the shepherds on that day of Christ's birth long ago...

Through all the centuries, history has vindicated His teaching...In this great country of ours has been demonstrated the fundamental unity of Christianity and democracy.

IN THE YEAR 1952 AD
KOREAN WAR

"FREEDOM IS NOT FREE" is the inscription on the Korean War Memorial in Washington, D.C. The Korean War ended July 27, 1953, with the armistice signed at Panmunjom. Begun three years earlier as a UN "police" action, the outnumbered U.S. and South Korean troops fought courageously against the Communist Chinese and North Korean troops, who were supplied with arms and MIG fighters from the Soviet Union.

With temperatures sometimes forty degrees below zero, and Washington politicians limiting the use of air power against the Communists, there were nearly 140,000 American casualties in the defense of the Pusan Perimeter and Taego; in the landing at Inchon and the freeing of Seoul; in the capture of Pyongyang; in the Yalu River where nearly a million Communist Chinese soldiers invaded; in the

Battles of Changjin Reservoir, Old Baldy, White Horse Mountain, Heartbreak Ridge, Pork Chop Hill, T-Bone Hill, and Siberia Hill.

First Lady Mamie Geneva Doud Eisenhower stated in a conversation at the Doud home regarding their son John Sheldon Doud Eisenhower, who was serving in Korea:

> He has a mission to fulfill and God
> will see to it that nothing will happen to him
> till he fulfills it.

The Korean War started June 25, 1950. Communist North Korea invaded South Korea, killing thousands. General Douglas MacArthur was given command of the U.N. Forces and after a daring landing of troops at Inchon, MacArthur recaptured the city of Seoul. Political involvement prolonged the war, resulting in high casualties.

On December 24, 1952, President Harry S Truman lit the National Christmas Tree, stating:

> Shepherds, in a field, heard angels singing: 'Glory to God in the highest, and on earth peace, good will toward men.'...We turn to the old, old story of how 'God so loved the world, that He gave His only begotten Son, that whosoever believeth in Him should not perish, but have everlasting life.'
>
> Tonight, our hearts turn first of all to our brave men and women in Korea.
>
> They are fighting and suffering and even dying that we may preserve the chance of peace in the world.

President Truman stated on Christmas, 1952:

> Our hearts turn first of all to our brave men and women in Korea. They are fighting and suffering and even dying that we may preserve the chance of peace in the world...
>
> Let us remember always to try to act...in the spirit of the Prince of Peace.
>
> He bore in His heart no hate and no malice - nothing but love for all mankind. We should...follow His example...
>
> As we pray for our men and women in Korea...let us also pray for our enemies...
>
> Through Jesus Christ the world will yet be a better and a fairer place.

General Douglas MacArthur led the United Nations Command in the Korean War from 1950 to 1951. He made a successful landing at Incheon, deep behind North Korean lines, and recaptured Seoul.

To the Salvation Army, December 12, 1951, General Douglas MacArthur said:

> History fails to record a single precedent in which nations subject to moral decay have not passed into political and economic decline.
>
> There has been either a spiritual awakening to overcome the moral lapse, or a progressive deterioration leading to ultimate national disaster.

IN THE YEAR 1955 AD
REV. MARTIN LUTHER KING, JR.

On December 31, 1955, Reverend Martin Luther King, Jr., pastor of the Ebenezer Baptist Church in Atlanta, Georgia, and founder of the Southern Christian Leadership Conference, led a nonviolent protest by boycotting the city buses of Montgomery, Alabama. Rev. King stated:

> If you will protest courageously, and yet with dignity and Christian love, when the history books are written in future generations, the historians will have to pause and say, 'There lived a great people...who injected new meaning and dignity into the veins of civilization.'

IN THE YEAR 1960 AD
DWIGHT EISENHOWER

President Dwight Eisenhower remarked in 1960:

> Through the ages men have felt the uplift of the spirit of CHRISTMAS. We commemorate the birth of the Christ Child by...giving expression to our gratitude for the great things that His coming has brought about in the world.

IN THE YEAR 1962 AD
"DO YOU HEAR WHAT I HEAR?"

There Really is a Santa Claus

In 1962, during the Cuban Missile Crises, the Christmas carol "Do You Hear What I Hear?" was written as a call for peace by Noel Regney and Gloria Shayne Baker:

Said the night wind to the little lamb,
"Do you see what I see?
Way up in the sky, little lamb,
Do you see what I see?
A star, a star, dancing in the night
With a tail as big as a kite."

Said the little lamb to the shepherd boy,
"Do you hear what I hear?
Ringing through the sky, shepherd boy,
Do you hear what I hear?
A song, a song, high above the tree
With a voice as big as the sea."

Said the shepherd boy to the mighty king,
"Do you know what I know?
In your palace warm, mighty king,
Do you know what I know?
A Child, a Child shivers in the cold—
Let us bring him silver and gold."

Said the king to the people everywhere,
"Listen to what I say!
Pray for peace, people, everywhere,
Listen to what I say!
The Child, The Child sleeping in the night
He will bring us goodness and light,
He will bring us goodness and light."

IN THE YEAR 1962 AD
JOHN F. KENNEDY

At the end of 1962, President John F. Kennedy stated:

We mark the festival of Christmas which is the most sacred and hopeful day in our civilization. For nearly 2,000 years the message of Christmas, the message of peace and good will towards all men, has been the guiding star of our endeavors...the birthday of the Prince of Peace...

To the one million men in uniform who will celebrate this Christmas away from their homes...and to all of you I send my very best wishes for a blessed and happy Christmas and a peaceful and prosperous New Year.

IN THE YEAR 1977 AD
JIMMY CARTER

President Jimmy Carter commented in 1977:

CHRISTMAS has a special meaning for those of us who are Christians, those of us who believe in Christ, those of us who know that almost 2,000 years ago, the Son of Peace was born.

President Jimmy Carter, seeking U.N. sanctions against Iran, December 21, 1979, stated:

Henry Longfellow wrote a Christmas carol in a time of crisis, the War Between the States, in 1864. Two verses of that carol particularly express my thoughts and prayers and, I'm sure, those of our Nation in this time of challenge...I would like to quote from that poem

'And in despair I bowed my head.
There is no peace on earth, I said.
For hate is strong and mocks the song
Of peace on earth, good will to men.
Then pealed the bells, more loud and deep,
God is not dead, nor does he sleep.
The wrong shall fail, the right prevail,
With peace on earth, good will to men.'

IN THE YEAR 1980 AD
SINGING IN SCHOOLS

United States Court of Appeals - 8th Circuit (1980), in the case of *Florey v. Sioux Falls School District*, 619 F. 2d 1311, 1314, 1315-1316, 1317 (8th Cir. 1980), stated that the performance and study of religious songs, inclusive of Christmas carols, is constitutional, provided the purpose is the:

Advancement of the students' knowledge of society's cultural and religious heritage, as well as the provision of an opportunity for students to perform a full range of music, poetry, and drama that is likely to be of interest to the students and their audience.

Advanc[ing] the student's knowledge and appreciation of the role that our religious heritage has played in the social, cultural and historical development of civilization.

It would be literally impossible to develop a public school curriculum that did not in some way affect the religious or nonreligious sensibilities of some of the students or their parents.

The study of religion is not forbidden "when presented objectively as a part of a secular program of education"....We view the term "study" to include more than mere classroom instruction; public performance may be a legitimate part of secular study...

As the district noted in its discussion of Rule 3, "To allow students only to study and not perform [religious art, music and literature when] such works...have developed an independent secular and artistic significance would give students a truncated view of our culture."

IN THE YEAR 1983 AD
RONALD REAGAN

Ronald Reagan stated in his Christmas Address, December 20, 1983:

Sometimes, in the hustle and bustle of holiday preparations we forget the true meaning of Christmas...the birth of the Prince of Peace, Jesus Christ...During this glorious festival let us renew our determination to follow His example.

President Reagan stated in 1983:

CHRISTMAS is a time...to open our hearts to...millions forbidden the freedom to worship a God who so loved the world that He gave us the birth of the Christ Child so that we might learn to love...The message of Jesus is one of hope and joy. I know there are those who recognize CHRISTMAS DAY as the birthday of a wise teacher...then there are others of us who believe that he was the Son of God, that he was divine.

IN THE YEAR 1985 AD
CHRISTMAS DISPLAYS

Warren Earl Burger (September 17, 1907-June 25, 1995), was Chief Justice of the U.S. Supreme Court, 1969-86. He had served on the faculty of William Mitchell College of Law, St. Paul, 1931-48; assistant U.S. Attorney General, 1953-56; and judge of the U.S. Court of Appeals, District of Columbia, 1956-69.

In a 1985 opinion of *Lynch v. Donnelly*, 465 U.S. 668, 673 (1985), Chief Justice Warren Burger upheld that the city of Pawtucket, R.I., did not violate the Constitution by displaying a Nativity scene. Noting that presidential orders and proclamations from Congress have designated Christmas as a national holiday in religious terms since 1789, he wrote:

The city of Pawtucket, R.I., annually erects a Christmas display in a park.... The creche display is sponsored by the city to celebrate the Holiday recognized by Congress and national tradition and to depict the origins of that Holiday; these are legitimate secular purposes.... The creche...is no more an advancement or endorsement of religion than the congressional and executive recognition of the origins of Christmas....

It would be ironic if...the creche in the display, as part of a celebration of an event acknowledged in the Western World for 20 centuries, and in this country by the people, the Executive Branch, Congress, and the courts for 2 centuries, would so 'taint' the exhibition as to render it violative of the Establishment Clause. To forbid the use of this one passive symbol...would be an overreaction contrary to this Nation's history.

There is an unbroken history of official acknowledgment by all three branches of government of the role of religion in American life.... The Constitution does not require a complete separation of church and state. It affirmatively mandates accommodation, not merely tolerance, of all religions and forbids hostility towards any....

Anything less would require the "callous indifference" we have said was never intended by the Establishment Clause. Indeed, we have observed, such hostility would bring us into a "war with our national tradition as embodied in the First Amendment's guaranty of the free exercise of religion."

IN THE YEAR 1992 AD
GEORGE H.W. BUSH

𝕴n his Christmas Message, December 8, 1992, President George H.W. Bush stated:

> As we celebrate the birth of Jesus Christ, whose life offers us a model of dignity, compassion, and justice, we renew our commitment to peace...Christ made clear the redemptive value of giving of oneself for others...
>
> The heroic actions of our veterans, the lifesaving work of our scientists and physicians, and generosity of countless individuals who voluntarily give of their time, talents, and energy to help others-all have enriched humankind and affirmed the importance of our Judeo-Christian heritage in shaping our government and values.

A.D. – ANNO DOMINI
YEAR OF THE LORD'S REIGN

ℭlarence E. Manion (1896-1983), was dean of the Notre Dame College of Law, 1941-52, and Professor of Constitutional Law at the University of Notre Dame, 1925-52.

Regarding the birth of Christ, Dean Clarence Manion commented:

> The long march of measured time suddenly stopped. It then did an about-face and started to march in another direction and to a different drum straight through the ensuing centuries of Christ and Christendom....
>
> B.C. (before Christ) and A.D. (Anno Domini, the year of our Lord) mark each one of the only reliable milestones along the path of world history. The end of the first time-chain, and the beginning of the second, came together on the night that Christ was born in Bethlehem.
>
> The first Christmas Day thus stands as the Great Divide for the timing and recording of all people, things and events that have lived or taken place upon this earth...
>
> It is the one place where an inquiring mind can go in either direction without stopping; the one place on the long, long trail of time where the magnetic needle of history stands vertical and points up.

BIBLIOGRAPHY

-From The Life, Service, Baathist, and Miracles of Saint Nicholas the Wonderworker, Holy Trinity Monastery Jordanville, NY. Holy Transfiguration Monastery, 278 Warren Street, Brookline, MA 02445-5997 USA (800) 227-1629 or (617) 734-0608 Fax: (617) 730-5783. Holy Transfiguration Monastery is under the Bishops of the Holy Orthodox Church of North America (HOCNA), which is a member of the Holy Synod of the True Orthodox Church of Greece.

http://home.attbi.com/~histotech2/saints.html&h= 225&w=169&prev=/ images%3Fq%3Dmyra%2 Blycia% 26svnum%3D10%26hl%3Den%26lr% 3D%26ie%3DUTF-8

-Eusebius, op. cit., VIII, ii, Eusebius, loc. cit., xi, xii; Lactant., "Div. Instit.", V, xi

-Catholic Encyclopedia, http://www.newadvent.org/cathen/05007b.htm, EUSEBIUS, Hist. Eccl. in P.G., XX; De Mart. Palæstinæ, P.G., XX, 1457-1520; LACTANTIUS, Divinæ Institutiones, V, in P.L., VI; De Mortibus Persecutorum, P.L., VII; GIBBON, Decline and Fall of the Roman Empire, xiii, xvi; ALLARD, Le persécution de Dioclétien et le triomphe de l'eglise (Paris, 1890); IDEM, Le christianisme et l'empire romain (Paris, 1898); IDEM, Ten Lectures on the Martyrs, tr. (London, 1907); DUCHESNE, Histoire ancienne de l'eglise (Paris, 1907), II. T.B. SCANNELL Transcribed by WGKofron With thanks to St. Mary's Church, Akron, Ohio The Catholic Encyclopedia, Volume V Copyright (c) 1909 by Robert Appleton CompanyOnline Edition Copyright (c) 1999 by Kevin KnightNihil Obstat, May 1, 1909. Remy Lafort, CensorImprimatur. +John M. Farley, Archbishop of New York

-Little Pictorial Lives of the Saints, a compilation based on Butler's Lives of the Saints and other sources, by John Gilmary Shea (Benziger Brothers: New York, 1894); Les Petits Bollandistes: Vies des Saints, by Msgr. Paul Guérin (Bloud et Barral: Paris, 1882), Vol. 14. Updated 08/14/2001 15:04:20.

-Saint Nicholas. ShonnieScarola, "St. Nicholas' Day, Domestic Church Communications, Ltd., Domestic-Church.com, http://www.domestic-church.com/CONTENT.DCC/19981101/SAINTS/nicholas.htm.

-Saint Nicholas. USA Today, December 23, 1997, Eric Brady, cover story, 1A-2A, (Gannett Co. Inc., 1000 Wilson Blvd., Arlington, Va 22229.

-Saint Nicholas. Domestic Church Communications, Ltd., Domestic-Church.com, http://www.domestic-church.com/CONTENT.DCC/19981101/SAINTS/nicholas.htm

-Saint Nicholas. http://www.rnw.nl/sinterklaas/en/flash/intro.html

-THE DAILY E-PISTLE IS A SERVICE OF: GGDWeb Developers, Inc., http://www.ggdweb.com; The Catholic Community Forum, http://www.catholic-forum.com The Catholic Forum offers an archive of past E-Pistles at: http://

/www.catholic-forum.com/e-pistle.html; Liturgical Publications of St. Louis, Inc. LPI St. Louis http://www.liturgical.com, 1-800-876-7000 or 314-394-7000, To receive a free subscription to the Daily E-Pistle, please visit: http://www.catholic-forum.com/e-pistle.html or send us an e-mail at newsletter@liturgical.com, Greg Dunn, Webmaster, The Catholic Community Forum, http://www.catholic-forum.com, Ben Dunlap, Editor, The Daily E-Pistle http://www.liturgical.com/cgi-files/maillist/s.cgi?r=1&l=9&e=

-Donne, John. 1625, in a message delivered Christmas Day. John Donne, LXXX Sermons, (1640), No. 3. John Bartlett, Bartlett's Familiar Quotations (Boston: Little, Brown and Company, 1855, 1980), p. 255.

-Tate, Nahum. 1700, in his Christmas Hymn, st. I. John Bartlett, Bartlett's Familiar Quotations (Boston: Little, Brown & Company, 1855, 1980), p. 317.

-Wilson, Woodrow. September 1, 1918, in a letter to Rabbi Stephen S. Wise in New York City, endorsing the Zionist Movement. A Compilation of the Messages and Papers of the Presidents 20 vols. (NY: Bureau of National Literature, prepared under the direction of the Joint Committee on Printing, of the House and Senate, pursuant to an Act of the Fifty-Second Congress of the United States, 1893, 1923), Vol. XVII, p. 8575.

-Truman, Harry S, Memoirs by Harry S. Truman-Volume Two: Years of Trial and Hope (Garden City, NY: Doubleday & Co, 1956), pp. 135, 136, 157.

-Thatcher, Margaret Hilda. February 5, 1996, in New York City, prior to her trip to Utah where she addressed the U.K. - Utah Festival, in an interview with Joseph A. Cannon, entitled "The Conservative Vision of Margaret Thatcher," published in Human Events - The National Conservative Weekly, (Potomac, Maryland: Human Events Publishing, Inc., 7811 Montrose Road, Potomac, MD, 20854, 1-800-787-7557; Eagle Publishing, Inc.), March 29, 1996, Vol. 52, No. 12, pp. 12-14.

-Bush, George Walker. December 10, 2001, lighting the White House Menorah for the first time,

-Winfred. The World Book Encyclopedia - 18 volumes (Chicago, IL: Field Enterprises, Inc., 1957), Vol. 3, pp. 1425-1426.

-Poinsett, Dr. Joel Robert. U.S. Minister to Mexico, 1825-1829. The World Book Encyclopedia - 18 volumes (Chicago, IL: Field Enterprises, Inc., 1957), Vol. 13, pp. 6439-6440.

-Truman, Harry S. December 24, 1946, in an address given at the Ceremony for the lighting of the national Christmas Tree. T.S. Settel and staff of Quote, editors, The Quotable Harry Truman, introduction by Merle Miller (NY: Droke House Publishers, Inc., Berkley Publishing Corporation, 1967), pp. 44, 57, 82, 115.

-Eisenhower, Dwight David. December 1954, remarks lighting the National Christmas Tree. James Beasely Simpson, Best Quotes of '54, '55, '56 (New York: Thomas W. Crowell Company, 1957), p. 78.

-Kennedy, John F. December 17, 1962, in an address given at the Pagent of Peace Ceremonies lighting the national Christmas Tree. T.S. Settel, editor, The Faith of JFK - introduction by Richard Cardinal Cushing (NY: E.P. Dutton & Company, Inc., 1965), pp. 125-127.

-Bush, George W. December 6, 2001, remarks lighting the National Christmas Tree, Office of the Press Secretary.

-Carver, George Washington. January 9, 1922, in a thank you note to one of his students, Mr. L. Robinson. Tuskegee Institute Archives, George Washington Carver Papers, reel 6, frame 1000. Gary R. Kremer, George Washington Carver - In His Own Words (Columbia, MO: University of Missouri Press, 1987), p. 85.

-Andersen, Hans Christian. Verses of "Barn (Child) Jesus," one of Denmark's best-known carols. Walter Ehret and George K. Evans, comps., The International Book of Christmas Carols (Englewood Cliffs, N.J.: Prentice-Hall, 1963), p. 193. Elizabeth Silverthorne, Christmas in Texas (College Station, TX: Texas A & M University Press, 1990), pp. 110-111.

-Washington, George. 1745, in some verses copied on "Christmas Day," at thirteen years of age. W. Herbert Burk, Washington's Prayers (1907), p. 12. William J. Johnson, George Washington - The Christian (St. Paul, MN: William J. Johnson, Merriam Park, February 23, 1919; Nashville, TN: Abingdon Press, 1919; reprinted Milford, MI: Mott Media, 1976; reprinted Arlington Heights, IL: Christian Liberty Press, 502 West Euclid Avenue, Arlington Heights, Illinois, 60004, 1992), p. 21.

-Franklin, Benjamin. William S. Pfaff, ed., Maxims and Morals of Benjamin Franklin (New Orleans: Searcy and Pfaff, Ltd., 1927)

-Manion, Clarence E. Statement. John D. Boland, Editor, Mindszenty Report (Cardinal Mindszenty Foundation, Eleanor Schlafly, publisher, 7800 Bonhomme Ave, P.O. Box 11321, St. Louis, MO 63105, December 1997), Vol. XXXIX, No. 12, p. 1.

-A Compilation of the Messages and Papers of the Presidents 20 vols. (New York: Bureau of National Literature, Inc., prepared under the direction of the Joint Committee on Printing, of the House and Senate, pursuant to an Act of the Fifty-Second Congress of the United States, 1893, 1923)

-Public Papers of the Presidents, U.S. National Archives and Records Administration, 700 Pennsylvania Avenue NW, Washington, D.C., 20408 http://www.archives.gov/, 1-866-272-6272, 301-837-0483 fax

-Irena Challmers, The Great American Christmas Almanac - A Compendium of Facts, Fancies and Traditions (Viking Penguin, Inc., a division of Penguin Books USA, 375 Hudson Street, New York, NY 10014, 1990)

Printed in the USA
CPSIA information can be obtained
at www.ICGtesting.com
LVHW050245080124
768378LV00008B/198